SUCCEEDING OUTSIDE THE ACADEMY

Succeeding Outside the Academy

Career Paths beyond the Humanities,

Social Sciences, and STEM

EDITED BY

JOSEPH FRUSCIONE

AND

KELLY J. BAKER

 University Press of Kansas

1048661673

Published by the University Press of Kansas (Lawrence, Kansas 66045), which was organized by the Kansas Board of Regents and is operated and funded by Emporia State University, Fort Hays State University, Kansas State University, Pittsburg State University, the University of Kansas, and Wichita State University

Library of Congress Cataloging-in-Publication Data

Names: Fruscione, Joseph, 1974– editor. | Baker, Kelly J., editor.
Title: Succeeding outside the academy : career paths beyond the humanities, social sciences, and STEM / Joseph Fruscione and Kelly J. Baker, eds.
Description: Lawrence : University Press of Kansas, [2018] | Includes index.
ISBN 978-0-7006-2687-8 (cloth)
ISBN 978-0-7006-2688-5 (paperback)
ISBN 978-0-7006-2689-2 (ebook)
Subjects: LCSH: College teachers—Employment—United States. | College administrators—Employment—United States. | Graduate students—Employment—United States. | Career changes—United States. | Doctor of philosophy degree.
Classification: LCC LB2331.72 .S85 2018 | DDC 650.14—dc23.
LC record available at https://lccn.loc.gov/2018027417.

British Library Cataloguing-in-Publication Data is available.

Printed in the United States of America

10 9 8 7 6 5 4 3 2 1

The paper used in this publication is recycled and contains 30 percent postconsumer waste. It is acid free and meets the minimum requirements of the American National Standard for Permanence of Paper for Printed Library Materials z39.48-1992.

To our families

CONTENTS

Acknowledgments, *ix*

Introduction, *1*
Joseph Fruscione and Kelly J. Baker

PART I: RECONSIDERING ACADEMIC CAREERS AND SUCCESS

1   Ten Things I Wish I'd Known during My PhD: How I Muddled My Way to a Great Career Anyway, *11*
Melissa Dalgleish

2   How to Move beyond the Professoriate, *23*
L. Maren Wood

3   Finding Footholds, Finding Your Way, *34*
Lisa Munro

4   How to Eat an Elephant; or, There's Life outside Academia, *44*
Rachel Neff

5   Run toward Yourself, *55*
Cathy Hannabach

6   What Would Your Poor Husband Do? Living with the Two-Body Problem, *67*
Kelly J. Baker

7   Reframing Success, *79*
Rachel Leventhal-Weiner

PART II: CREATING NEW CAREERS

8   Manifesto: The Freelance Academic, *93*
Katie Rose Guest Pryal

9   Faculty Development: The (Unnecessarily) Long and
    Winding Road, *105*
    Lee Skallerup Bessette

10 You Never Know: From Professor to (UX) Professional, *115*
    Abby Bajuniemi

11 How I Left My PhD in English Behind and Learned to Love
    the Stacks, *127*
    Brian Flota

12 Education, Writing, Entrepreneurship: Creating Impact
    through Communities, *139*
    Rusul Alrubail

13 Finding the Fulcrum, *149*
    Jessica Carilli

14 Can I Do This? Do I Want To? Building a Career in Real
    Estate, *159*
    Elizabeth Keenan

    Epilogue: Unhappy Beginnings, *170*
    Joseph P. Fisher

    About the Contributors, *177*

    Index, *183*

ACKNOWLEDGMENTS

We want to thank Joyce Harrison and the University Press of Kansas for thinking this project was publishable and valuable. Thanks also to all the folks at the press who made this book that you are now reading.

A lot of people helped make this book possible. Joe is losing track of all the smart people in, around, or beyond academia he's engaged with regularly on Twitter: Derek Attig, Kevin Gannon, Shonda Goward, Katie Anderson Howell, Chris Humphrey, Nyasha Junior (#selfcare), Trent Kays, Karen Kelsky, Carly Lesoski, Amy Lynch-Biniek, Chuck Pearson, Jen Polk, Melissa Richard, Andrew Robinson, Rebecca Schuman, Liana Silva, Carol Tilley, John Warner, and Kate Weber. Everyone involved in making this book. We're always connecting and always learning from each other. This book wouldn't exist without Twitter. Early in the process, Hollis Baguskas, Taylor Bryant, Shannon Cate, M. G. Gainer, and Katie Wedemeyer-Strombel gave Joe great feedback about what they—as current or former academics—wanted in a book like this. He hopes they get what they wanted. Extra thanks go to Kat Jacobsen for her graphic design skills, work on the unicorn chart you'll soon see in the Introduction, and general awesomeness. Kristen and Henry continue to make his family life lively, interesting, and indispensable.

Kelly wants to thank all those amazing people who directed her to take an alternative-academic path and suggested she could imagine new career options, if only she were brave enough to try. Many of those folks Joe already mentioned above. And yet, Lee Skallerup Bessette, Betsy Barre, Derek Attig, Jen Polk, Liana Silva, Richard Newton, Martin Kavka, Chuck Pearson, Heather Nicholson, Rachel Christensen, and Josh Eyler were particularly helpful to her. Katie Rose Guest Pryal proved to be an excellent sounding board in each stage of this book and responded to Kelly's texts and calls like a champ. Cheryl Strayed's *Tiny Beautiful Things* (2012) clarified the importance of building a life, not just a career, and shifted the way Kelly approached the world. It's a book she returns to again and again to figure out what life throws at her, so you should all read it too. Her parents, Dottie and Steve Raines, and sisters, Stephanie Basford and Ashley Slesser, and brother, Cary Barfield, have been supportive of all her career shifts and reimaginings. Her children, Kara and Ethan Baker, haven't always been the most help, but they make sure that she takes time for fun beyond work, even if it includes impromptu dance parties in her office. Her partner, Chris Baker, is a tireless supporter of all of her endeavors, in work and life. She couldn't have finished this book, or any other book, without him.

And thanks to you, the reader, who picked up our book. We hope it helps you imagine a career and a life outside academia. Actually, we just hope that it helps.

SUCCEEDING OUTSIDE THE ACADEMY

Introduction

JOSEPH FRUSCIONE AND KELLY J. BAKER

Not every PhD becomes a professor. Some never wanted to be one in the first place. Some tried and struck out on the market. Others thought they wanted to be a professor and then found a more fulfilling path. We don't know how many PhDs thought being a tenure-track professor was the only acceptable job, but many of us believed this during and after graduate school. Call it the *Tenure Track or Bust* mind-set. A job with tenure or nothing at all awaited us, or so we thought. This mind-set has affected many current and former PhD students, leading some of us to think that not getting a tenure-track job made us professional, and personal, failures.

What we didn't know at the time was that the odds were stacked against us before we took our first course. Academic hiring practices have changed dramatically since the mid-1970s. Adjunct and other part-time positions used to be largely reserved for full-time professionals moonlighting as professors to share their expertise. Now, such positions are essentially required for many ABDs and PhDs to gain teaching experience, but these positions are not necessarily steps forward on the path to a tenured position. Contingency is the new normal in higher education.

As of 2011, the American Association of University Professors (AAUP) documented that 70 percent of academic faculty were non-tenure-track (NTT).[1] Using data from 2009, the Coalition of

---

1. John W. Curtis, "Trends in Faculty in Employment Status, 1975–2011," March 20, 2013, American Association of University Professors, https://www.aaup.org/sites/default/files/Faculty_Trends_0.pdf.

Percentage Increase of Employees in Higher Education Institutions from 1975–1976 to 2011. Source: For 1975 and 1976, National Center for Education, *Fall Staff in Postsecondary Institutions*, 1993, and *Digest of Education Statistics*, 2001. For 2011, National Center for Education Statistics, *IPEDS Human Resources Survey* 2011–2012, Fall Staff Component. Provisional data file. Tabulation by John W. Curtis.

the Academic Workforce (CAW) claims 75 percent.[2] For the last forty years, tenured positions have declined while contingent positions have increased. PrecariCorps, a nonprofit foundation aiding adjuncts, adapted the AAUP data into a chart that showed part-time NTT faculty increased 286 percent and full-time NTT faculty increased 259 percent since 1975. Full-time tenured and tenure-track faculty increased by a slight 23 percent, and full-time executive positions increased by 141 percent. This is the market that PhDs of the 1990s and early 2000s faced.

The 263-point difference between tenure-track and part-time faculty job growth is unconscionable. It's also not accidental, given the massive uptick in senior administrative positions—and salaries—in the modern university. Due to various systemic failures in academia and graduate education, many PhD students from the 1990s through the 2000s simply weren't prepared for

2. The Coalition on the Academic Workforce, "A Portrait of Part-Time Faculty Members," June 2012, http://www.academicworkforce.org/CAW_portrait_2012.pdf.

nonacademic careers. (Some were barely prepared for academic careers, as many of our writers show.)

Yet contingent work didn't affect all academics equally. Women and people of color are more likely to end up off the tenure track and in contingent work. Marisa Allison, a researcher for New Faculty Majority Foundation, uncovered a problematic trend: the rise in contingent labor happened alongside the rise of women in doctoral-degree programs.[3] And, writing for *Slate*, Tressie McMillan Cottom, an assistant professor of sociology at Virginia Commonwealth University, writes that African American academics are 50 percent more likely to not land a tenure-track job. While Cottom noted the growing concerns in higher ed about "adjunctification," she documented that Black faculty and students have been protesting the "ghettofication of Black scholars in adjunct roles" since at least the 1960s.[4] Hand in hand with such skewed hiring practices is academia's bias toward young, "fresh" PhDs. Our contributor L. Maren Wood has done some excellent, much-needed research on who gets tenure-track jobs.[5] Despite what some humanities and social sciences PhDs might think—and hope for—their age and experience work against them on the job market. As Wood's data have shown, the farther a PhD is from their degree, the less hirable they seem. The majority of recent tenure-track hires in humanities and social sciences have either gone to ABDs or PhDs within two years of their degree. The hiring window closes dramatically after that. Long-time adjuncts are at a disadvantage. Many of us simply aged out of the system.

When starting our professional journeys in academia, we wanted all those innovative courses, articles, conference presentations, and valuable service work to parlay themselves into tenure-track jobs. *Of course,* we thought, *all this great work won't go unnoticed—or unrewarded. All these CV lines will add up to a full-time position. I'll keep at it.* All those CV lines added up to a lot of things: student loan debt, contingent positions, unpayable credit card bills, frustration, heartache, and feelings of failure. *What's wrong*

3. Gwendolyn Beetham, "The Academic Feminist: Advocating for Contingent Faculty's Rights with Marison Allison," *Feministing*, October 14, 2013, http://feministing.com/2013/10/14/the-academic-feminist-advocating-for-contingent-facultys-rights-with-marisa-allison/.

4. Tressie McMillan Cottom, "The New Old Labor Crisis?" *Slate*, January 24, 2014, http://www.slate.com/articles/life/counter_narrative/2014/01/adjunct_crisis_in_higher_ed_an_all_too_familiar_story_for_black_faculty.html.

5. L. Maren Wood, "Who Lands Tenure Track Jobs?" Beyond the Professoriate, December 2, 2016, https://lilligroup.com/2016/12/02/who-lands-tenure-track-jobs/.

with me? we asked ourselves. *I'm doing everything right; I'm following my advisers' advice.*

Then we started thinking about things differently: *Hopping from lectureship to visiting professorship isn't a career; it's professional limbo. Maybe academia doesn't deserve me. What else is out there for me? What else can I do?*

Many PhDs have left teaching—or academia altogether—for different work: some in alternative-academic (alt-ac) careers and others outside academia entirely. Our seventeen contributors essentially trained themselves in their new fields because their graduate programs provided little (if any) career guidance for anything except being a scholar. We chose our writers because of their credentials, supportive attitudes, and career variety:

- Rusul Alrubail: education writer and speaker
- Abby Bajuniemi: user experience researcher and designer
- Chris Baker: director of engineering at a startup
- Kelly J. Baker: freelance writer and editor of *Women in Higher Education*
- Lee Skallerup Bessette: instructional technology specialist
- Jessica Carilli: federal scientist
- Melissa Dalgleish: career, professional development, and grants specialist
- Joseph P. Fisher: lecturer and assistant director of Disability Support Services
- Brian Flota: academic librarian
- Joseph Fruscione: editor, proofreader, and writing consultant
- Cathy Hannabach: editor and consultant for interdisciplinary academics
- Elizabeth Keenan: real estate agent
- Rachel Leventhal-Weiner: data specialist and policy analyst
- Lisa Munro: academic editor and writing coach
- Rachel Neff: digital strategist and freelance writer, editor, and indexer
- Katie Rose Guest Pryal: freelance writer, editor, and lawyer
- L. Maren Wood: career coach and researcher

Our contributors document how to develop a career from a diversity of vantage points. Most are PhDs who show how transferable our skills can be. That is not necessarily the message that's usually provided to PhD students and other junior academics, who are typically siloed into one field or subfield. We can have trouble seeing past our specific knowledge to the more general skills we gained from teaching and research. Some also followed the *Do what you love* and *Teaching is a calling, so don't worry about money* platitudes often espoused by those in privileged positions. Many of us had to either learn from our mistakes or pay consultants to show us how to be an effective academic, or alternative-academic, jobseeker. Those of us who left academia had to learn about our new career paths on the fly because we were rarely, if ever, shown any other way.

Succeeding Outside the Academy hopes to change this.

We've asked readers like you who've been through a PhD program to imagine if, in addition to having guest scholars lecture about their research, you also had guest speakers explain, discuss, and hold a workshop to help train you for different careers. Our guest lecturers are not professors talking to the next generation of scholars or telling them to hang in there and keep applying for professorships. They're writers, editors, or translators. Maybe they're programmers or designers. Perhaps they freelance while working or parenting full-time. Or they've carved out their own career niche. Instead of talking about a recent book they've written or some research topic, they'll discuss their field and show you concrete ways to start finding a different kind of job in a market with considerably greater growth potential.

It's a simple concept—offering PhDs diverse job training—yet it's not as common as we'd like to see. Our contributors tell their stories and then offer practical, relatable, and repeatable advice for transitioning into alt-ac positions. Each contributor writes about

- how they've gotten to where they are
- what they would have liked to hear (or learn) when finishing grad school and entering the academic market
- what they've learned from their struggles
- the specific steps readers can start taking.

This approach allows our contributors to both share their experiences of what they had to learn on their own and give practical advice to help you start your own alt-ac career journey. They address several issues: how they got started; how they draw on academic training while doing the work each day; how they reworked their approaches to writing, deadlines, and collaboration; and how they distilled useful, transferable skills from the specific knowledge they gained in academia. They also offer the kind of information and advice that many tenured faculty aren't able to give. They're up-front about the struggles and successes they've encountered. Honesty, given the current state of academia, is *Succeeding Outside the Academy*'s most important objective.

If you have (or are about to have) a PhD and want to know what career options you have besides being a professor, then you're holding the right book. If you work in the academy advising graduate students, then you're holding the right book. If you're a longtime adjunct realizing you'll only ever be a longtime adjunct, then you're holding the right book. *Succeeding Outside the Academy* offers options beyond the academic positions you've trained for and shows how contributors built the careers, and lives, they now have. Our writers use clear, accessible, and concrete language to model the kinds of writing done in alt-ac or nonacademic fields. In giving you necessary preparation for different kinds of careers, they'll address the types of work you have to do. In essence, our writers describe their journeys from academia to other employment—and then provide a map of the tasks along the way so you can follow a similar path, such as

- assessing their skills
- marketing themselves and networking
- learning how to be entrepreneurs
- handling interviews and salary negotiations
- learning to write specific documents (e.g., cover letters, résumés, pitches, professional bios, cold-call emails, reports, and freelancing policies)
- drawing on academic training while doing the work each day.

Our writers discuss what they had to learn about the alt-ac job market on their own, and then they'll help you start learning the same things. They'll also share their struggles and failures, since knowing what didn't work can be just as instructive as what did.

At least four contributors address academia's two-body problem, which both points to entrenched sexism in higher education and shows how complicated the academic job search can be for partnered women. It's hard not to notice that most of our contributors, thirteen out of seventeen, are women, which suggests that gender still deeply matters in who succeeds in academia and who doesn't. It's also important to note what this collection suggests about race and academic careers. Most of our contributors are white, and so are most of the faculty at institutions nationwide. As of 2015, 77 percent of full-time faculty at colleges and universities were white: 42 percent were white men, and 35 percent were white women. The other demographics suggest deep racial imbalances in hiring and promotion. The rest of full-time faculty included 6 percent Asian/Pacific Islander men, 4 percent Asian/Pacific Islander women, 3 percent Black women, 3 percent Black men, 2 percent Hispanic women, 2 percent Hispanic men, and up to 1 percent American Indian women and men.[6] Structural racism is a problem that the modern university has yet to solve.

Ultimately, our writers are the experts. They've written as if they're running a workshop for grad students and fresh postdocs. Given this chance, they'll tell you about their alt-ac job searches and share what they would have wanted to learn while in their PhD programs. *Succeeding Outside the Academy* addresses how, as our colleague M. G. Gainer described it when we started this book, alt- and post-acs are not failures but adapters. This journey is about adapting to different fields, needs, and challenges. Since changing careers is not always a seamless transition, we're not simply offering success stories but showing you the work you have to do—and that it's not easy. Academia, as many know, is not necessarily conducive to building a life. This book emphasizes how readers can build lives (not just careers) and emphasize other priorities (not just academic goals). We've all had to adapt and continue adapting.

Succeeding Outside the Academy is a book for anyone who got limited guidance on careers outside academia. In graduating scores of students unprepared for anything except a tenure-track job, PhD programs have created the stigma of being a "failed" academic who leaves higher ed. Many new and would-be alt-acs have no idea how to navigate a new job search, network, and learn industry expectations. Some also equate not getting a tenure-track job with personal failure.

We want to change this. Our writers show you examples of another life and career, as well as *how* to get them. In a word, we're offering hope. Hope that your knowledge and training are broadly useful. Hope that a rich, supportive community awaits you. Hope that, while academia punishes your experience, other fields and industries reward it. And hope that you can build a better, more fulfilling life after leaving academia.

6. National Center for Education Statistics, "Fast Facts: Race and Ethnicity of College Faculty," 2017, https://nces.ed.gov/fastfacts/display.asp?id=61.

PART I

Reconsidering Academic Careers and Success

I

Ten Things I Wish I'd Known during My PhD

How I Muddled My Way to a Great Career Anyway

MELISSA DALGLEISH

Back in 2011, when I decided that I was never going to go on the tenure-track job market, the bountiful career support for PhDs that can be found at the touch of a smartphone did not exist. I found myself scouring the web (between despairing sobs) in search of shreds of hope and help, as there was none to be found in my graduate department or at my university (or so I thought).

Not knowing what I could do with my PhD was anxiety-inducing and painful. Not only was I facing the loss of my identity as an academic, but it also didn't feel like there was anything better—or anything at all—waiting for me on the other side.

I found what information on graduate career development I could, and I went on with my usual PhD pursuits—teaching, research, writing—although with considerably more anxiety, and less motivation, than before. Then the Faculty of Graduate Studies at my university went looking to buy out someone's teaching assistantship so that person could write a white paper on graduate professional and career development. Still hedging my bets on the academic job market, I was nervous about giving up a year of teaching. I applied anyway and offered up what I knew in an interview. I got the job and then spent a year researching what was available at my university, and across North America, to help PhDs move into what we now call alt-ac (alternative-academic, or non-faculty, or post-ac, or just plain old) careers.

At the end of the year, I presented my white paper to the more than fifty graduate department chairs at my university with the aim of getting buy-in for creating an institution-wide professional and career development program. I recommended, as a start, that the university create a core professional and career development program open to all graduate students and a task force of students, faculty, and staff dedicated to coming up with ways to better support the majority of graduate students who would not become faculty.

Their response? "Our students don't need a graduate professional development program. They don't need career support. They're all going to become professors."

Sigh.

I went back to my research and writing, but with a much better grasp of what was actually available on campus for graduate job seekers—far more than I had thought in my despairing days—and a much better idea of what I wanted my career to look like. Through my white paper research, I'd found some models of what an amazing post-PhD career could look like: an English major who did user experience design for Google, a sociologist who had started his own market research firm, a biochemist who helped fund tech startup companies, and so on. I'd also found tools and resources—the self-assessments in the books *So What Are You Going to Do with That?* and *Strengthsfinder 2.0,* the myIDP tool, stories about the paths others had taken told in the forums on Versatile PhD—that were helping me figure out what I was good at doing, what I liked doing, and the kinds of careers that contained lots of both.

On Facebook one day shortly after that project ended, a friend shared a posting for a role in the faculty I had just left, managing graduate research funding and coordinating the few professional development workshops the Faculty of Graduate Studies then offered. My self-assessments had taught me that I valued supporting lots of research more than focusing only on my own, that I was great at coordinating activities and people, and that I would do best in jobs where I would have opportunities to both write and teach. This job offered all of that.

But the posting was closing the next day. And I didn't have a résumé because I hadn't been planning to start job hunting for at least another year. In a mad scramble, I put together an application. Over the next few weeks, I interviewed and then was offered the job.

(I should pause here for a moment. I hate to disappoint you, but my pathway into a nonfaculty career isn't at all typical—we don't have great research on this, but what we do have suggests that it takes on average about five years to settle into a post-PhD career. Promise me you won't compare your career trajectory with mine and feel like you're doing it wrong!)

A year later, I launched the university-wide graduate and postdoctoral professional skills program I had started to build by writing that first white paper, a program that continues to serve more than 6,500 students and post-docs.

I've since moved on to run the professional and career development program at a medical research institute affiliated with the University of Toronto, the largest university in Canada. I know a lot more about science, and about the specific challenges that STEM students face, than I did before. I've also had half a decade to watch my students and fellows move into—and flourish in—all kinds of careers: policy analysis, communications, pharmaceutical research, management consulting, project management, research administration, event planning, finance, human resources, journalism, publishing, and just about anything else you can think of.

A significant part of my job is helping students and fellows like you—along with the graduate-trained job seekers who read my writing online or work with me on their job applications—understand the academic and nonacademic job markets, learn how to be strategic about their professional and career development, and give themselves the best options and odds for finding a career that rewards them personally and financially.

Basically, I do for them what I wish someone had done for me during my own PhD.

This is advice that you might also find useful, whatever stage of graduate or post-PhD life you're in. So, I'm going to share with you the ten key things I wish I had known when I decided not to become a professor, the ten key things—from learning what being a professor is really like to making room for serendipity—that all graduate students should do during their degrees to prepare themselves for awesome post-PhD lives. It's the advice I wish I'd gotten before embarking on my own PhD, despite having muddled my way to a great career anyway.

1. Understand Why You're Doing a PhD and Choose Your Graduate Program Wisely

Why are you doing a PhD? And how might that "why" influence where you choose to do it?

I'll be blunt: if you're going to graduate school because you want to become a professor, make sure that you only accept admission to an elite university (on full funding), as your chances of getting a tenure-track role if you study anywhere else are vanishingly small.[1]

But if you're doing a PhD for another reason—you want to spend five to eight years exploring a topic you find fascinating, you're treating your PhD like a limited-term job that doesn't pay terribly well, you're interested in a nonfaculty career in which PhDs are valued—you've got some other choices to make.

One of them is whether or not you should do a PhD at all—I'd say *don't* unless most of the above is true. But if those things are true, and you're really committed to doing a PhD, here are some questions you should ask of graduate programs before you accept an offer of admission, and some rules I'd advise all graduate students to follow:

- Is the program fully funded? (Don't go into debt for a PhD.)
- Does the program recognize and celebrate graduates who have moved into nonfaculty jobs? (Don't go somewhere you'll be considered a second-class citizen.)
- Will you have a variety of opportunities to develop skills that will be useful outside the academy? (Don't limit your learning to the classroom.)
- Is your prospective supervisor supportive of a range of career goals? (Don't hide what you want.)
- Will there be other students in your cohort who are also aiming at (or at least open to) a career in something other than the professoriate? (Don't go it alone.)
- Is this the best place to learn what you want to about your dissertation topic, even if it's not the best place to become a professor? (Don't settle.)
- Is this somewhere you (your partner? your kids?) want to live for the next five to eight years? (Don't forget about the rest of your life.)

If you want to keep your career options open after a PhD and pursue both academic and nonacademic jobs, you're going to be looking for an elite program that supports a variety of career goals. They do exist! And it's possible to shift the culture of a less open program once you get there. But if you're not interested in the professoriate, you have a

1. Joel Warner and Aaron Clauset, "The Academy's Dirty Secret," *Slate*, February 23, 2015, http://www.slate.com/articles/life/education/2015/02/university_hiring_if_you_didn_t_get_your_ph_d_at_an_elite_university_good.html.

whole world of options when choosing where to spend the next years of your career.

2. Understand the Reality of What Comes after Grad School

Research shows that more than 80 percent of graduate students start their PhDs expecting to become tenure-track professors.[2]

Guess what?

Nowhere near 80 percent of PhDs actually end up in tenure-track jobs. Most estimates suggest that fewer than 50 percent of PhDs end up in any kind of academic job (that includes contract teaching) and only 15–25 percent ever secure tenure-track positions.[3] That is, sadly, the reality. I very much hope that this doesn't come as a shock and that the graduate programs you applied to, and the one to which you accepted an offer of admission, shared its alumni placement information with you at an early stage.

Even if you chose a graduate program because it was going to help you become something other than a professor, it's really easy to forget what you came for. The culture of many graduate departments is such that regardless of what people want when they start the PhD, they end up absorbing—often unconsciously—the idea that they're working toward (and capable of) becoming one thing and one thing only: a tenured professor. That wasn't what I was aiming for when I started—I just wanted to hang out and

2. Among respondents to Katina Rogers's "Humanities Unbound" study, 74 percent anticipated becoming professors at the beginning of graduate school; Desjardins's study pegs that number at 65 percent overall and somewhat higher in the humanities (as in Gregory Brennen's 2013 study, which pegs the number at 83 percent). See Katina Rogers, "Humanities Unbound: Careers and Scholarship beyond the Tenure Track," Scholars' Lab, April 23, 2013, http://scholarslab .org/research-and-development/humanities-unbound-careers-scholarship-be yond-the-tenure-track/; Louise Desjardins, "Profile and Labor Market Outcomes of Doctoral Graduates from Ontario Universities," Culture, Tourism and the Centre for Education Statistics, July 2012, http://www.statcan.gc.ca/pub/81-595-m/81 -595-m2012098-eng.pdf; and Gregory Brennen, "Evolving Value of the Humanities PhD: The Motivations, Expectations, and Perceived Values of PhD Study in the Humanities," June 2013, https://humanitiesphd.files.wordpress.com/2014/01 /brennen_evolvingvaluereport_websiteversion_1-7-13.pdf.

3. See Conference Board of Canada, "Where Are Canada's PhDs Employed?" November 24, 2015, http://www.conferenceboard.ca/press/newsrelease/15-11-24 /where_are_canada_s_phds_employed.aspx and the American Survey of Earned Doctorates, https://sedsurvey.org/.

learn things for a few years—but I totally absorbed the message that that was what I *should* want.

Don't do what I did.

You need to prepare for, and embrace, the multitude of possibilities open to you after you complete your degree. And you need to remember that being an academic is just a job, and that there are tons of interesting, fulfilling jobs doing an infinite number of things. Otherwise, you may end up disillusioned and disappointed when you don't get the thing you didn't even want in the first place. You may also end up making decisions—to take low-paid, low-security work as a way to stay in the academy, for example—that aren't in your best interest in the long term.

3. Think about What You Really Want to Do

If you want to become a professor, answer a question for me: When you made the decision to go to graduate school, how much did you really know about the life of a professor? How much about it do you really know now?

That life is almost never what people think it is. And their decision to pursue that career is based on incomplete information.

Parts of the academic life match up closely with the starry-eyed dream I had as a young graduate student—engaged students, exciting research discoveries, time to read and write—but others definitely don't. I had to make the effort to figure out what those parts were, what the reality of being a professor is actually like. Meetings are endless and often frustrating. Grading is a slog. The pressure to publish, win grants, and get stellar teaching evaluations can be debilitating. Tenure denials happen. Students are disengaged. Service takes up far more time than people realize. Academic and administrative priorities clash. There's never enough time for research and reflection. Departmental and university politics can be fierce. Grants can run out and jobs disappear along with them.

Is that really what you want? Or just what you think you want?

Regardless of what you want to do after your PhD, you should be using your degree to figure out what you really love about academia and thinking about jobs that will let you do those things most of the time. The perfect job is one in which you get to do the things you're good at most of the time for reasons you can get behind and for a salary that makes you feel secure.

That might be an academic job. Or it might not.

The other important part of this process is to talk to people you know in academia and outside it and find out from them what their jobs are *really* like. So long as we perpetuate the belief that academia is the only worthy place of employment, and that a professorship is the only truly fulfilling and engaging job, you and other graduate students like you might ignore a whole host of career possibilities that might be a much better personal and professional fit.

I often recommend the book *So What Are You Going to Do with That?*, which includes some fantastic exercises to help you figure out what you're good at, what you like doing, and where you can do those things with a PhD. Tools like myIDP (for STEM researchers) and ImaginePhD (for humanities folks) are also a great place to start. Diagnostic tools like these helped me realize that the things I love to do and am good at doing—coordination, strategy, communications, writing, mentorship, process improvement—are key components of all sorts of jobs, including my current one. I've also found ways, as many PhDs do, to continue the parts of my academic life—research, writing, publishing—that I find rewarding in addition to the job that pays me.

And I can tell you with great certainty: I'm far happier and more engaged as a researcher in my current career than I would have been as a professor.

4. Think about What You Really Don't Want to Do

As PhDs, many of us are indoctrinated to believe that we should be willing to give up everything for a tenure-track job. At some point, I shrugged this off and made a list of the things that were more important to me than tenure: I didn't want to move across the country, wait until I was forty to have kids, spend most of my life grading papers, spend multiple years as a contract professor, or write things that no one would ever read. For me, those were pretty convincing reasons to give up on the idea of becoming a professor, which requires near total mobility, constrains reproductive choices, requires far more teaching than research, and values journal and book publications that almost no one ever reads.

I had to convince myself that choosing where to live, when to have children, how I wanted to be treated and paid by my employer, and what audience I wrote for were totally legitimate life choices.

And I had to do this in the face of an academic culture that made me feel that if I wasn't willing to sacrifice my whole life—even my whole identity—to being an academic, I was a second-class citizen. But I did it, and in return I ended up with a job that I love and that pays well in the city where all of my family and friends live, a job that leaves me with the time, energy, and inspiration to write all kinds of things, for all different audiences.

I also never have to grade another paper!

5. Explore What Makes You Curious

As a friend kindly reminded me after I kept claiming that I got lucky in ending up in my job, we make our own luck. What seems random is actually a series of decisions to explore what makes us curious, or to do something outside our normal routines and plans, that leads to a whole host of post-degree opportunities. Career development folks call this "planned happenstance," and it's a concept you might find useful. Planned happenstance involves

- figuring out what interests you
- training yourself to ask "How can I?" rather than saying "I can't because..."
- preparing to jump on unexpected opportunities
- taking action—to learn, develop new skills, meet new people, and explore new opportunities.

Basically, you stop planning your path forward. Instead, you plan for how you'll take action when unplanned opportunities present themselves, and then see where they take you.

I didn't know what planned happenstance was when I embarked on my own unplanned career path, but I had figured out what interested me, and I was willing to open myself up to possibility. Knowing that I was curious about graduate career development, I paid attention when a job posting went out for a research assistant (RA) who would write a white paper on the topic. My instinct was to say, "I can't because . . . no one will take me seriously on the academic job market if I lose out on a year of teaching experience." But I quashed that impulse and then asked myself, "How can I explore and share what I know about how PhDs get jobs and how the university can support them?"

By taking the RA job, obviously.

As I did my RA work, I learned a ton. I also developed skills like researching nonacademic topics, writing for a general audience, working with university administrators, and navigating large, complex organizations. I met dozens of new people across the university whom I would never have had the chance to meet otherwise. I also got a full-time job and a career I love directly from that little research assistantship—planned happenstance at its finest. (And even if

I had decided to pursue a professorial job, the work I did and connections I made while writing that white paper would have been highly useful.)

There are more and more opportunities available to graduate students that will let you explore what makes you curious: taking a research position with a professor doing something totally different from your dissertation research, doing work for an administrative unit of your university, pursuing an industry-partnered dissertation project, going on an international exchange, choosing a graduate program that includes co-op placements, or volunteering with a community group. Find what appeals to you, make sure it pays, and take action. Meet new people. Learn new things.

You never know where it will lead you.

6. Take Advantage of the Resources Available on Campus

As grad students, it's easy to believe that most of the student support services available on campus are there for undergraduates, but that is emphatically not the case. There are myriad resources available on most campuses to help graduate students make the most of their degrees, to help them navigate the academic job market, or to help them transition into a nonfaculty career.

The career center is a great place to start, and staff can provide assistance with academic and nonacademic job searches. Alumni relations can often connect you with alumni in the fields you're interested in. Many universities now have graduate student professional development programs that offer a whole host of workshops and seminars, and programs like Mitacs and MyGradSkills (both Canadian, but there are similar US programs) offer a full suite of free transferable-skills workshops.

And surprisingly, many faculty members can provide guidance and support in the search for jobs inside *and* outside the academy. Some of them have significant nonacademic career experience; others have broad networks outside the academy. (It can be scary talking to your supervisor about your plans to abandon the tenure track—believe me, I know—but the culture of silence around career transition and nonfaculty job searches won't fully disappear until we all start talking about it.)

7. Consider Creating a Shadow CV

In order to demonstrate to people outside the academy that you have the skills and experience they want, you must provide evidence that you're capable of working outside the academy.

Seems obvious, right?

Especially for PhDs, the assumption that we're overeducated and lacking in practical skills can be hard for employers to overcome without seeing evidence of our nonacademic experience. In addition, having nonacademic work experience can go a long way toward helping you mentally connect the skills you've honed as a graduate student with those that crop up on job postings, and to help overcome the feeling that there's nothing you're qualified to do but be a professor.

Some people have started calling experience developed alongside academic work, but not included in academic documents, a "shadow CV." You might know it better as a side hustle. In my case, I took a year off between my master's degree and my PhD to work in publishing, and I tutored high school students and took the occasional editing job during my PhD. Other people I know have done summer placements, taken part-time jobs, done industry-partnered internships, or created web-based consulting and writing firms that allow them to work on their own time. For all of them, their shadow CV work was a key part of their post-PhD job search success.

8. Learn How to Talk about Your Skills and Research to People outside Academia

Academese and English can sometimes seem like two different languages. Unsurprisingly, our tendency to use specialized language and technical terms (also known as that ancient evil, the dreaded jargon) makes it hard to translate our qualifications and research into terms that make sense in contexts outside the academy.

It's only natural.

Communicating highly specialized research to nonacademics isn't a skill that many academics, at any level of seniority, practice all that much. (Well, other than the inevitable attempts to explain your work to your mother, or to someone you meet at a party.) But opportunities to practice do exist, and you should take advantage of them: compete in a Three Minute Thesis competition. Take workshops on clear language writing. Blog about your research for the nonacademic people it might matter to. Connect to people who aren't academics on Twitter.

Writing and speaking in plain language can seem odd to grad students, especially those of you who have been in academia for a long time, but once you learn how to do it, the relationship between what you do as an academic and what shows up in job postings often becomes painfully obvious. Your work in designing protocols for your lab and overseeing projects starts to look a whole lot like process improvement and project management. You realize that being good at teaching and publishing has value as oral and written communication skills. Once you've started to realize how the rest of the world might understand and benefit from your research, its potential impact outside the academy becomes clearer, which can open up new avenues of career exploration in areas related to your academic research. As a side benefit, granting agencies are increasingly looking for evidence of the ability to communicate research beyond the academy.

9. Don't Conflate Who You Are with What You Do

This is hard to avoid in the current culture of academia, but if you can avoid the trap of believing that you *are* an academic, and that if you don't continue to work as an academic you'll be nothing, you'll save yourself a horrible and painful identity crisis when the professoriate becomes an unattainable dream.

I should know. I've been through it. It is not fun.[4]

Embarking on a new career path is hard enough—don't make it worse by having to fashion yourself a new identity at the same time. Tying your identity to being an academic also tends to close you off to other opportunities and possibilities in graduate school that may be important for your success later. It's also hard to convince a hiring manager that you're genuinely interested in the job they're offering if you still think of yourself mostly in academic terms. Why should they hire someone who seems to be waiting for the academic job they really want and will leave if it comes his or her way?

So remember this: You are not an academic. You are an interesting, intelligent, flexible, creative person who at the moment does academic work. And if you end up doing other work, you'll still be all those things. A professorship is just a job. It is not a vocation or an identity, and you are so much more than the limited career options and identities the academy tells you are worthy.

4. You might find the research and writing of Herminia Ibarra, a professor of organizational behavior at INSEAD, interesting. She researches how people form identities based on their work and what strategies work best for rebuilding those identities when moving onto a new career path. Her book, *Working Identity: Unconventional Strategies for Reinventing Your Career*, is a good place to start.

10. Enjoy the Ride

Getting paid to read for your qualifying exams.
Taking classes totally outside your area because you can.
Auditing things purely for interest.
Debating theory over far too much wine.
Choosing conferences based on where you get to travel.
Making friends you never would have met otherwise.

These are some of the best parts of grad school, and they should be relished, and they often aren't because PhDs are too busy conferencing and publishing and professionalizing and shadow-CV-ing and comparing themselves to all the other PhDs they know. Yes, those things need to get done (minus the last one), but statistically speaking, the chances of getting to stay in academia on a permanent basis are slim.

Enjoy the ride while it lasts.

But don't worry if and when it comes to an end. What comes next is even better.

2

How to Move beyond the Professoriate

L. MAREN WOOD

In 2004, I moved from Canada to the United States to start my PhD in American history at the University of North Carolina at Chapel Hill. I was elated. Carolina is a top-ten program in history. When I started, most alumni went on to tenure-track jobs, which was my dream. In the 2008–2009 academic year, the final year of my program and my first year in the job market, the Great Recession hit. It was chaos. Jobs were being pulled faster than they were being posted. One week I had an interview at the annual American Historical Association meeting, but a week later the search committee chair called to say the job was canceled. That happened to almost everyone I knew who was on the job market that year.

Advisers assured me that the job market would "improve," and I decided to keep at it: to teach, publish, and submit job applications. To pay my bills, I worked as a research associate, writing a digital textbook, and taught courses as an adjunct. By the summer of 2011, I was burned out. The kicker was coming in second for a three-year teaching position, which would have necessitated living across the country from my partner while teaching three classes a semester for $35,000 a year. The professoriate no longer looked promising. Instead of the middle-class lifestyle I hoped to secure by earning a PhD, I faced employment insecurity and low wages.

Like many PhDs, I internalized the failure to land my dream job. Even though I knew the job market had collapsed, I still thought, somehow, with hard work and perseverance, I would secure a rewarding position as a tenure-track professor. But there are simply not enough jobs for all the talented people, and it is brutal to be the one culled from the academic community. Most who earn PhDs are star students who have been rewarded for their hard work within academia. They have won prestigious awards and postdoctoral fellowships, have had articles published, and have been encouraged by friends and mentors, all along surpassing others in their cohorts in terms of accomplishments, accolades, and awards. Then, when they enter the job market, the strategies they have used to be successful no longer work. That can be profoundly destabilizing to their sense of self.

The summer of 2011, as I faced my decision to stay or leave academia, I went home to visit my family. I grew up on the Wood family farm in Southern Alberta, where my parents and my grandfather (now ninety-five) still live. The farm was purchased by my great-grandparents, Harold and Ida Wood, and my grandfather lives in the original farmhouse once inhabited by his parents. During my visit home, I went to see my grandfather. As I opened the door to his home, I began reflecting on the events that had brought my family to this piece of land almost a century ago.

Before acquiring the farm, Harold was a sheep rancher and butcher. For much of the year, the family lived in the middle of nowhere on a ranch north of Taber, Alberta; it is still in the middle of nowhere. To find the ranch requires GPS and my grandfather's impeccable memory.

Harold and Ida did not own the sheep ranch. They lived in a dilapidated shack on the side of the creek and spent winters in a rented house in town. One winter, all their sheep froze to death. With her oldest sons growing up "wild" on the ranch and the loss of their livestock, Ida insisted that the family move closer to Taber, where her children could attend school and church on a regular basis.

In 1927, Ida and Harold purchased a farm about two miles south of Taber, an enormous achievement in the days before credit was widely available. They dug the basement and framed the upstairs of a modest farmhouse, but there was no money to complete the upstairs. Harold, Ida, and their seven children moved into the basement.

Three years later, their oldest son, Ray, who had gone away to agricultural school, died suddenly at the age of nineteen. The stock market had crashed, and the "dust bowl," which encompassed much of the midwestern United States, extended north into Saskatchewan and Alberta. Throughout the 1930s, the Woods had little cash, but my grandfather often remarked that the family was "lucky" because the farm had irrigation and they always had food.

Then, World War II came and Ida and Harold sent three sons off to war, including my grandfather. During the war, building materials were scarce,

Wood family sheep ranch. Family photo contributed by author.

and so it was not until the mid-1940s, after spending nearly twenty years living in the basement, that Harold and Ida finished their home and moved upstairs.

The house Harold and Ida lived in is now my grandfather's home. A photo of that sheep ranch hangs on his living room wall.

As I stood in my grandfather's living room looking at that picture and reflecting on the history of the house and land on which I stood, I thought—whose dream was that? To live in a shack on the side of a creek, isolated from everyone; lose a child; raise a family in a basement; live through a depression and war? In that moment, things came into perspective for me. No, I was not going to be a professor, and in the grand scheme of world events, that was not as big a tragedy as it felt to me in the moment. What is more, I—the great-granddaughter of a sheep rancher and farmer—had already achieved so much. What I needed to do was stop dumping my time and talents into a career path that was leading nowhere, stop lamenting shifting economic conditions I could not control, and move forward in a new direction.

As it turned out, coming to that realization was the easiest part of my journey into a post-academic career. In December 2011, I left North Carolina and moved to Washington, DC, to join my partner, who had taken a job in consulting. I arrived depressed and listless. While I needed to move forward, I had no idea how or where to begin. Who was I if I was not a historian, an academic? What were my interests outside of teaching and history? What motivated me? What were my skills? And what kinds of careers were of interest? These were questions I had never asked of myself before, and I was ill-equipped to find the answers.

As a result, my job search was a total disaster. Looking back with the eye of a career coach, I can see that "2012 Maren" made every mistake in the book. It is this process of failing, learning, and recalibrating that motivated me to start Beyond the Professoriate to help fellow PhDs avoid the pitfalls and mistakes I made.

What are the most common mistakes I, and most PhDs, make when they start a nonfaculty job search?

- *We assume that our credentials matter.* After all, what is the point of a PhD if it does not open doors? The truth is, outside a small number of STEM and social sciences disciplines where people develop specialized technical skills, few of us will find a job that *requires* a PhD. Employers are looking for a combination of knowledge, skills, and abilities, and less at education and credentials. The good news is, as a PhD you have an impressive range of skills and abilities, but chances are you have no idea which of your skills are in demand nor how to communicate your value to an employer.
- *We focus on writing résumés and submitting them to online job postings instead of networking.* This is, in part, because we learn job search strategies from academics. The approach taught in my department graduate seminar was standard: we spent early fall crafting a job letter, teaching statement, and research statement. We made sure our CVs listed absolutely all our accomplishments and teaching experience. Then we hit the job boards. In history, jobs are listed on the academic jobs wiki, where you have the added benefit of reading all the gossip and internalizing everyone else's stress. It is an anxiety-inducing nightmare.

When you submit your materials for a tenure-track job, you might modify the job letter a bit, but not a lot, because it has been "perfected" through multiple drafts read by faculty in the department. And your professional documents are *long*. A two- to three-page cover letter is standard. A CV of less than four pages seems light. Then there is the teaching statement, the research statement, the sample syllabi, transcripts, teaching evaluations, and an article or draft chapter. It is not uncommon to send upward of sixty pages for one job application.

For a position beyond the professoriate, you will submit a one-page cover letter and a two-page résumé, for a grand total of three pages. Occasionally, a hiring manager might ask for additional materials or have you complete a test.

In an academic job search, we do not value networking. Perhaps, if your adviser knows someone in the hiring department, she will send an email or pick up the phone, advocating for her student. Maybe someone from your program was hired a few years earlier, and your adviser might reach out and put in a good word. It is rare in academia to apply for a job where you, the candidate, have a solid connection based on your own network.

For a job search beyond the professoriate, it is extremely difficult to land a job without having a personal connection to someone within the organization. By some estimates, as many as 70 percent of jobs are filled through networking, and as many as half of jobs are never posted. If you are relying on job boards instead of speaking to people who work at organizations of interest to you, you will miss most opportunities.[1]

On the rare occasion that someone who is already teaching as an adjunct or visiting assistant professor at that institution, or someone with a degree from a university with several alumni already on faculty lands an academic job, we roar with rage on the academic jobs wiki about the unfairness of an internal hire. Rightly or wrongly (and I think wrongly) the academic job market is imagined to operate on merit—international job searches to find "the best" candidates. This is not true, but it is how candidates are trained to think about the academic job market.

But hiring someone internally, or a candidate with a recommendation from someone who works within the organization, is standard and considered smart in almost every other industry. Hiring is time-consuming and expensive, and firing someone is difficult. If a colleague assures me that Candidate X is a good fit for the organization, that personal reference is probably all I need to bring that candidate in for an interview. Most likely, if the candidate does well in that interview, I am going to hire him or her. That is not nepotism; it's effective hiring. Why risk hiring an unknown?

If employers care more about skills than education, if most jobs are not posted, and if people are hired because they have a personal connection to the organization, then how do you, the PhD leaving academia, launch a *successful* job search?

1. Kimberly Beatty, "The Math behind the Networking Claim," *Jobfully Blog*, July 1, 2010, http://blog.jobfully.com/2010/07/the-math-behind-the-networking-claim/.

I. CREATE A METRIC TO MEASURE OPPORTUNITIES BY
IDENTIFYING YOUR MOTIVATORS, INTERESTS, AND VALUES.

We often skip this step and move right into résumé writing, but it is important to reflect on your interests because you have the skills to do many things, but you might not like doing them. You may have the skills to be a grant writer; you may also hate every minute of it.

Usually, when I ask PhDs what they like to do, they say, "I like teaching" or "I like research." Okay, but why? What motivates you in your work?

- Analyzing, inquiring, and researching?
- Helping and empowering others?
- Social justice?
- Creative insights?
- Originality?

I have clients complete a Strong Interest Inventory, which you might be able to take through your university career center. There are also many free inventories you can find online to help you articulate your interests outside your narrow academic specialization. As a historian, I like studying people and cultures, and I enjoy investigating and applying my findings to solve problems. These broad interests brought me to the field of history; they are not confined to it. By identifying the interests that brought you to your field of study, you can begin to imagine other places where you might find similar (or more!) satisfaction.

If inventories are not of interest, try an exercise called "Seven Stories," which many career coaches use. Think of seven moments in your life—from your earliest memory to the present—when you felt energized, inspired, and successful. What were you doing? Write these down and then review them. What patterns emerge?

Some clients prefer creating a vision board. This is a pictorial representation of your ideal life. When you imagine yourself at work, what are you doing? Are you speaking in front of an audience? Winning an award for groundbreaking research? Working with a team? Writing alone? Where do you want to live? What kind of home do you want to live in, and who will you share your space with? Find pictures and make a poster that you can display near your workspace. The job search is challenging, and it can be useful to have a visual reminder of what you are trying to achieve.

2. LEARN TO TALK ABOUT WHAT YOU DO INSTEAD OF WHAT YOU KNOW.

When we ask an academic what "they do," they often answer by saying what they study. For example, when people used to ask me, "Maren, what do you do?" I would respond with, "I study representations of sexualities in early American print culture." That sounds simultaneously salacious and useless to most employers. More to the point, it is not at all what I *do* in terms of tasks, skills, competencies, and abilities.

Remember, most people come into contact with a PhD once in their life, as an undergraduate sitting in a college classroom. Few people know what goes into designing and teaching a college-level course, writing a dissertation, conducting community studies, or running a lab. It is up to you, the job seeker, to tell them.

Take out your academic CV and make a list of everything you do in a day. The main categories on a CV are usually teaching, research/publications, grants and awards, and service to the profession. Take teaching as an example. It is the beginning of the semester, and you are teaching a new course. You start by writing a syllabus. But what goes into creating a new syllabus? What decisions do you make? How do you select readings? What steps do you take to write a lecture? Deliver a lecture? Answer student emails or run office hours? Grade and provide feedback on papers? When you have finished listing every task you do as part of teaching, move on to other parts of your CV.

3. ONCE YOU HAVE AN INVENTORY OF YOUR TASKS, REPACKAGE THEM INTO KEY SKILLS AND CORE COMPETENCIES.

Skills are the abilities we leverage to effectively perform a specific activity or job, such as writing, computer programming, or speaking in front of an audience. Competencies are underlying characteristics, behaviors, and skills, such as analytical thinking, conflict resolution, creative thinking, and interpersonal relations. There are many free resources online that can help you learn about core competencies, but one book I recommend is *Competency-Based Resumes* (2004) by Robin Kessler.

The key to a successful job search is to think of yourself as a package or cluster of interests, subject matter expertise, and core competencies. These should be things you are good at and enjoy doing and can allow you to bring value to a variety of organizations. Do not think of careers as "doctor, teacher, lawyer, or dentist." That is too limited of a way to think of careers in the twenty-first-century creative economy. Today, few people stay in the same job, or with the same employer, for more than a few years. To move up, to advance in their careers, or to stay employed requires them to stay nimble. If you think of yourself in terms of a unique collection of skills and abilities, you can find opportunities with a range of employers, enhancing your employability.

4. RATHER THAN FOCUSING ON SPECIFIC JOB TITLES, FOCUS INSTEAD ON ORGANIZATIONS WHERE SOMEONE WITH YOUR SKILL SET, CORE COMPETENCIES, AND INTERESTS CAN BRING VALUE.

To do this, read company websites, job advertisements, and employee profiles on LinkedIn. What is the mission statement of the organization? What do they help their clients / partners achieve? What key skills and competencies do they value in their employees? What skill sets and competencies do employees highlight in their LinkedIn profiles or company bios? For PhDs with strong qualitative analytical skills, you are conducting a rhetorical analysis to help you understand the language, values, and goals of a new audience—employers of interest. If you tend to be a quantitative thinker, you might use an Excel spreadsheet to keep track of key words and then run a simple pivot chart. What is in demand?

5. ONCE YOU HAVE A CLEAR UNDERSTANDING OF THE LANGUAGE AND VALUES OF ORGANIZATIONS OF INTEREST, AND A CLEAR SENSE OF YOUR OWN CORE COMPETENCIES, IT IS TIME TO START WRITING PROFESSIONAL DOCUMENTS.

Oftentimes, PhDs talk about converting a CV into a résumé, but that's a failed strategy. A CV is based on accomplishments and is often sent without revision to multiple job ads. A résumé, however, must show your unique combination of skills and core competencies, and speak to the specific needs of the employer. While you should have a master résumé document, any résumé that you submit for a job must be carefully edited to the criteria outlined in the job ad.

Most professionals in career transition use a combination résumé to highlight key skills and core competencies while also providing a sense of career history. Hiring managers do not want functional résumés because they do not provide a sense of a career history, and a traditional chronological résumé will only show that you lack linear work experience.

Résumés are forward-looking documents. This may seem nonsensical because you are writing about your work history, but the goal of a résumé is to show what you *can do* based on what you have done. It is a persuasive document carefully crafted to convince someone that you are the right person for a position. Anything that does not serve this goal needs to be removed. When you include something on a résumé—publications, grants, or awards—ask yourself, "What skill / competency does this demonstrate, and will the employer find it of value?"

Ask yourself this same question when including information from your work history. If your new career path is in communications, then only include research experience to the extent that it is relevant, perhaps to demonstrate project and time management. Your future employer will be much more interested in the hundreds of hours you spent designing and delivering lectures, speaking to a room of experts, or writing and editing the department newsletter than the fact you wrote a 300-page dissertation.

Adopt the language of the employer. If a position requires strong leadership skills, do not expect the employer to know that a good teacher is a good leader. Instead, describe your teaching as leadership. Calling people in your classroom "students" brands you as a teacher; saying you have "facilitated 200+ hours of small group discussions with twenty to thirty participants" sounds like someone who could run team meetings. Do not lie, do not exaggerate, but do translate your work experience into language that is understood by people in your new career field.

6. ONCE YOU HAVE A PENULTIMATE RÉSUMÉ, TURN YOUR ATTENTION TO YOUR ONLINE PROFILE.

A successful job search strategy involves reaching out to new people to ask for informational interviews. Many of these asks will come via LinkedIn. LinkedIn has an array of videos and tutorials to help you get started and make the most out of that platform. Learn to love LinkedIn.

A LinkedIn profile includes a summary profile statement where you describe who you are as a professional; you may choose to use this space to talk about your transition from academia to your new career. You would not include this on a résumé or cover letter, but it is appropriate on LinkedIn.

As a template, use profiles of people working in your chosen field. Include your work history, as you did on your master résumé, using keywords familiar to employers and colleagues. Unlike on a résumé, you can use first-person pronouns and full sentences on LinkedIn.

7. THERE IS NO NEED TO CREATE OR MANAGE A SEPARATE
   BLOG OR WEBSITE; UPLOAD MEDIA, POST RELEVANT
   PUBLICATIONS, AND WRITE A PROFESSIONAL BLOG
   DIRECTLY ON THE LINKEDIN PLATFORM.

The people you want to reach will be on LinkedIn, and managing a website and trying to drive traffic to it is time-consuming.

What you write and share on LinkedIn should be of value to the people in your network. If you want to transition into health policy, start writing about health policy. Share news stories or white papers with your network, and include thoughtful comments and analysis. This will show people you are serious about your career transition and highlight your research and communication skills.

Make sure that your online presence reflects your new professional identity. Perform a quick Internet search on your name and minimize, delete, or make private any account or post that distracts from your new image as a working professional in a new field. If you are strongly branded as an academic (you have a website that showcases your articles and teaching for an academic job search), consider taking it down. If you are political on Twitter, consider making your profile private, unless you are applying for positions where a strong political opinion would be considered an asset.

8. NOW THAT YOU HAVE A CLEAR SENSE OF HOW YOU
   WILL PRESENT YOURSELF IN PERSON, ONLINE, AND IN
   PROFESSIONAL DOCUMENTS, YOU ARE READY TO START
   NETWORKING AND LOOKING FOR OPPORTUNITIES.

It is important to remember that networking is not synonymous with self-promotion. If all you are doing is talking about yourself and hustling people for jobs, then you are not networking. Networking is about building relationships; it is about listening, connecting, solving problems, and creating community.

Start by telling people you already know—former students, friends, family, acquaintances—about your career transition and asking them to introduce you to people they know in this field. Once you have exhausted your current network, you can begin reaching out to new people for informational interviews.

An informational interview is exactly what it sounds like: an opportunity for you, the job seeker, to learn more about a person, their organization, the career field, and opportunities. It is *never* an opportunity to ask directly for a job. Asking people to speak with you for thirty minutes over coffee or on the phone is common outside academia, and many people will agree. Keep in mind that successful professionals are connectors; they have an extensive network of colleagues they can call upon. You are letting people know you exist and what your skills are, and that allows them to make use of your talents. So, reach out.

In an ideal situation, you will build contacts at an organization through networking, and then when a job is posted, you can reach out to your contacts to let them know you will be applying for the position, and ask if they have any specific recommendations or insights to help you in your application. Hopefully, they will put in a word to the hiring manager. An even better scenario is that your contact tells you about an upcoming position and invites you to apply.

Another benefit of informational interviews is that you will learn about trends in the field and the workings of specific organizations, and gain insights into the day-to-day responsibilities of different types of jobs. When you apply for a job, or interview, you will have a much better understanding of the needs of the employer and how you can add value.

Those are my top tips for job searching beyond the professoriate. It will take time, perhaps six months or longer, but you will be successful if you keep at it. You may have to take an entry-level position, volunteer, intern, or work as a contractor before landing a full-time job. That does not mean that your investment in your education was a waste; once you learn the ins and outs of your new career field, you will be able to advance. The PhDs who speak on career panels for Beyond the Professoriate all testify to this.

My parting piece of advice is this: *Do not think you have to know what you want to do for the rest of your life before you leave academia.* Think about what you want to try next. Most likely, what you try next will be but a temporary stop in your career path. You might try something and hate it; you might try something and love it but not where you work; you might decide you love where you work but not your specific job. These are all normal parts of a career transition, and it will probably take several years for you to settle into a new career path. But think of how exciting this is! You will learn, take on new challenges, and meet new people who can challenge the way you think and how you approach the world. For me, being an entrepreneur is a rollercoaster. Every day I learn new things. Now, instead of speaking to historians and fellow academics, I collaborate with people who are trained in business, engineering, marketing, communications, and online learning, as well as with graduate students, deans, faculty, and PhDs in career transitions. I find this challenging but exhilarating.

If you are someone who loves learning, solving problems, and meeting people who think differently than you do, then a career beyond the professoriate will be rewarding and satisfying.

3

Finding Footholds, Finding Your Way

LISA MUNRO

After many long, hard years of work, you're about to submit your dissertation and finish your PhD. After you graduate, you're looking forward to getting a full-time tenure-track job as an assistant professor at an important university in a nice city. You've done all the right things to make that happen: you've gone to the right conferences, met the right people, and published in the right journals.

You begin applying for tenure-track jobs in earnest. You're a better candidate now that you've finished the dissertation. You craft meticulous two-page cover letters printed on official department letterhead. You draft inspirational teaching statements that emphasize co-created knowledge and get glowing letters of recommendation from influential faculty about your potential as a scholar. You write a job talk about the cutting-edge nature of your research and hold mock interviews with department faculty. You're ready.

You send away your application packages online and in hefty manila envelopes that cost a lot of money to mail. You keep track of all your job applications on a complicated spreadsheet.

You wait.

You check the academic job wiki regularly and watch as other people receive interviews at top universities. You're still waiting. Most of the search committees ghost you, not bothering to send proper rejection letters or even emails. When they do send a rejection letter, they send it a year later, as if you didn't notice that they didn't want to interview you.

You've got a total of two short-list interviews out of the forty-nine job applications you submitted. You go to your annual meeting, held at fancy hotels in an expensive city far away. Your department will reimburse you $200 of the $1,500 you've spent on the "discounted" conference-rate hotel room and the cheapest flight you could find. You charge everything to your credit card, wondering how you'll pay it off. You wear your only suit and totter around in heels a bit too high. Search committees interview you in their hotel rooms while you perch on strangely sized loveseats and try to seem professional. At the end of the hiring season, you have not been invited back for a single campus interview.

Your student loan lenders start sending you threatening emails about repaying your six-figure student loan that accrues interest daily. The grace period is only six months.

You start to panic. *This can't be happening*, you think. Good students still get tenure-track jobs. People keep telling you that the market will improve. They don't say when. They advise you to keep applying and to be patient. You're running out of money.

You think maybe you'll need to work your way into a tenure-track position. So, you apply for the least awful adjunct jobs even though they require a 4-4 teaching load (four classes a semester in the fall and spring) and don't offer health insurance. You also apply for one-year postdocs at random universities you've never heard of, located in places where you definitely don't want to live. And then, suddenly, you realize that those options aren't real jobs. They're glorified temp jobs, the kind you might get at your local employment agency, just with fancier names. They pay about the same amount.

Congratulations. You've just graduated with a PhD in the humanities. You're unemployed. You can't believe it. This is your life.

In 2008, the global economic recession crushed the academic job market. That collapse sent shock waves through every institution of higher education. Although the crash affected all disciplines, including the social sciences and STEM fields, the humanities suffered most of all. Focused on finishing my master's thesis in history, I didn't notice that academic jobs had vanished overnight. I was too infatuated with my research to think about the practical and economic realities of the demise of the academic job market. In 2009, I continued into the PhD program without much thought about future (un)employment possibilities.

In 2013, as a shiny new all-but-dissertation (ABD), I started applying to academic jobs. I was a good student and had worked hard in an excellent graduate program, so I assumed I'd get a tenure-track position. I'd heard rumors about the dearth of tenure-track jobs and the growing adjunct crisis from colleagues, but believed that the economic realities of the job market applied to everyone but me. My department faculty assured me that the job market was "getting better," even though it wasn't. I didn't receive a single job interview my first season on the academic market, much less an actual job. I received two short-list interviews the following year. I was not invited to any on-campus interviews. I racked up an impressive list of rejection letters and an even longer list of job applications submitted to search committees who never bothered to respond at all.

Finally, after a few years on the academic job market, I conceded defeat. I was not going to get an academic job. I'd done all the right things but felt like I'd failed to find the holiest of academic grails: the tenure-track job at an R1 (Research 1) university. My academic career was over before it had even started.

I also had absolutely no backup plan.

My department, skilled in the art of getting students into academic jobs, seemed unprepared to help its students figure out what to do when they didn't get those jobs. My graduate cohort and I were left on our own to try to craft new careers out of the remaining shreds of our dignity and damaged self-esteem. Unsure of what else to do, I visited my university's career center. I had an awkward chat with a career counselor who didn't seem to understand why I could no longer pursue an academic job. I tried to explain that I needed the tools to create a new career path because I didn't know where to start. Career services referred me to some online skills assessments tests and outdated career exploration books that suggested to me that based on my work history and education, I would be well suited to be a history professor. I wanted to scream.

When I decided to leave academia for good in 2015, no instruction manual existed. I cobbled together ideas, searched out like-minded people, and took many wrong steps. Creating a meaningful life and new career outside academia has been anything but a linear narrative of progress, but I'm healing and headed in the right direction. I want to share with you what I've learned from the process in the hopes of making your transition out of academia less terrifying and more joyful.

First, if you've decided to leave academia, congratulations!

Second, you probably feel that you're in crisis. It's awful.

You've just sailed right off the map of your known world, and nothing looks familiar. You might feel terrified, disoriented, and confused. Life feels uncertain, crazy, chaotic, frightening, and painful. Or you might feel grief, rage, and shame. You might not even be able to imagine ever feeling happy again or how you will ever make enough money to pay off your huge student loan.

Your greatest moment of crisis, however, is also your greatest moment of opportunity. You now have a chance to reinvent your life in a way that fits you. You get to create some new goals that help you pursue your specific dreams and passions, rather than ones that other people and institutions have defined for you. It's like being a teenager again, with all the possibilities and opportunities but without the angst-filled poetry.

But first you have to remember who you are and what you want. Start with some deep self-reflection, because self-knowledge is self-power.

After years of gliding along a well-worn track that seamlessly guides you from graduate student to tenure-track job, you may have forgotten who you really are. Your identity crisis might feel even greater if you've been going to school since you were six and now you have a PhD. School may feel like not just what you do in life, but who you are. Your understanding of who you really are may have gotten buried under your academic persona. The academic you wanted to be led you to believe that one, and only one, acceptable job choice and personal identity lies at the end of your journey: the tenure-track professorship.

That is bullshit.

The world is bigger than academia. The world outside universities has many interesting problems to solve that need your heart, creativity, passion, and thinking skills. In fact, your greatest talents may be best applied to things that have nothing to do with academia. Academia, for all its big ideas, might actually be too *small* to contain you, your talents, and your dreams.

Academia has defined your goals and priorities for so long that it's hard to remember that other possibilities even exist. Stepping outside academia feels terrifying because of the sheer number of choices you now face. Nonacademic careers don't have clearly marked milestones and predefined goals; they begin with a confusing array of choices and pathways that lead in different directions. Which way should you turn? You may feel overwhelmed, bewildered, and so paralyzed by fear that you don't know where to start.

You'll find your first foothold when you remember what you truly love in life. What do you love most? Think hard and reach deep. You may assume that teaching is the thing you love most. However, I'm willing to bet that teaching isn't your only or even greatest love in life, even if years of school have told you otherwise. What other things ignite a tiny spark within you? Do you hear the little voice inside you that whispers, *Come this way*? You and your dreams matter, but you've got to remember what they are first.

I have never met a child who wanted to grow up to be a tenure-track professor. Before school convinced us that our dreams weren't important, we wanted to be veterinarians, astronauts, firefighters, scientists, explorers, movie stars, or ballerinas. We might have even invented jobs that didn't exist in the real world. Maybe you think back and find that buried under all of the academic stuff is a passion for photography. Maybe you feel the most engaged and excited about life when you're wandering on a mountaintop. Maybe somewhere deep within you is a dream to fly around the world solo. Maybe you want to make and create art. Maybe nothing in your life makes sense except your intense love of plants. Maybe you discover that you secretly crave celebrity and want to be a singer.

While figuring out my dreams, I concluded that I loved three things: writing, living abroad, and history.

As a kid, I dreamed of being the youngest person ever to publish a book. (Spoiler alert: it didn't happen.) I wrote short stories. I was also an aspiring journalist and created my own newspapers, illustrated with blurry, under-developed, 1980s Polaroid photos. When I was nine, I invented a kid's text-book about writing. As a teenager I wrote tortured poetry and even worse short stories, but it didn't matter, because I was doing what I cared about most.

In my late twenties, I'd served as a Peace Corps volunteer in Guatemala after finishing my undergraduate degree in history. I lived there again for two years while doing my dissertation research. I also lived in Mexico for a year while I finished writing my dissertation. I didn't want to just travel; I wanted to deeply know and understand certain places. I loved learning about the cultures of the people I met. I loved speaking Spanish. Even though I was a foreigner in those places, I felt much more at home abroad than I ever did stateside. I felt challenged to explore and grow in new ways every day. I wanted those experiences to be a part of my daily life.

I also thought a lot about what I wanted to take away from my graduate studies. I loved writing history. I still think of myself as a historian because I think like a historian. However, I hadn't started graduate school to become a professor. I went to graduate school because I had an intense desire to understand the world around me. I loved studying history and thinking about how to use history to better understand the world. I concluded that just because I had decided to leave academia, I didn't have to burn down everything on my way out of town.

Turns out, none of the things I love the most have anything to do with being a tenured professor.

While you're figuring out your new life goals and remembering your dreams, spend time thinking about what you don't love and what you want less of in your life. Maybe you started working at a nonprofit and realize that its mission doesn't reflect your values. Maybe you thought you wanted to be a freelance writer, but the rollercoaster nature of it freaks you out. Maybe the structure of a job and a boss and a cubicle and a time clock just doesn't work for you. Maybe you've swallowed your PhD pride and you're working a series of weird jobs at a temp agency and you're bored making spreadsheets all day for minimum wage. Maybe you hate your first new day job in sales.

That's okay. It's all just feedback. You're learning about you. The more you know about yourself, the better choices you'll make about your post-academic life. Once you know what you value and love, as well as what you don't, you can start thinking about where you might find those things in the world. You'll also be better equipped to avoid jobs and careers that absolutely won't work for you.

My first few steps outside academia taught me a lot about what I didn't want in a career, which eventually helped me define what I did want. At first, I worked as a temp at a job that a lot of people would have jumped at the chance to have: a nonprofit devoted to promoting the art and science of craft brewing. Working with the craft brewing industry sounded cool, but my heart wasn't in it. I worked in a cubicle. The office was noisy, and I had to pack noise-canceling headphones with me every day. I made a lot of spreadsheets. The people involved in craft brewing were mostly white guys with beards in their thirties; their problems didn't feel urgent to me. While I was there, a job opened up and I applied, but it wasn't a job I actually wanted. I felt a sense of relief when I received the rejection email.

When the beer job ended, I got another temp job where I did audio transcription; I sat at a computer for eight hours a day and made notes about audio clips. The work felt mind-numbing and boring. Because the work involved listening to audio, I had no chance to talk to anyone else in the office. I felt isolated, lonely, and angry. I discovered that I had zero tolerance for doing work that I didn't care about. I also needed intellectual stimulation and human connection.

As a side gig, I started doing freelance editing for humanities scholars. I liked helping people improve their writing. I enjoyed watching my clients use my suggestions to shape their projects into terrific articles, theses, and chapters. But I couldn't stand the ups and downs of freelancing. Some months I had a lot of work, and other weeks I was wondering if I had enough money left in my checking account to buy groceries. I felt stressed and desperate.

I needed some steady income, so I took a job as a crime victim advocate. I liked going out on crime scenes and talking with victims. I felt privileged to step into people's lives and deep traumas and to offer them care and support. Nevertheless, I found that I missed intellectual life, books, knowledge, and writing. I missed creative work and living overseas. I struggled with having a boss after years of working independently with minimal supervision. I also didn't love teamwork or endless meetings.

After much self-reflection to discover my values, my purpose, who I was, and what I really wanted in life, the pieces of my personal career puzzle were these:

- *Purpose*: helping people understand the world and themselves better
- *Values*: creativity, curiosity, place, community, healing, expression, education, teaching, freedom, flexibility, independence, exploration, mindfulness, engagement, personal growth, challenge
- *Oh Hell No*: cubicles, nine-to-five, boss, financial instability, isolation, work that I don't care about, teams, meetings, grant writing, schedules, time clocks
- *OMG Yes*: writing, living abroad, and history.

Based on all the above, I've come up with a new life plan: living my best and most creative life in Mexico. Writing, as always, remains front and center. It can't, however, be my only job because the ups and downs of free-lancing make me dizzy. In addition, I'm planning to host writing retreats for people who need time and support to get their creative work done. I want to offer writing retreats specifically for people to write about trauma and healing. I want to help people tell their stories in ways that feel meaningful and empowering to them. I also want to start teaching outside classrooms and sharing my love for Latin America, its people, and its history with others. I'm planning to offer specialized walking tours in Mexico that inspire critical thinking and engagement with the past and involve local people. My biggest dream is to create a study-abroad program for both students and nonstudents.

Entirely independent of academia, I've defined new goals and designed a life plan that works for me. I'm now focused on building bridges to reach my new goals every day. And truthfully, my plan sounds like a whole lot more fun than sitting in a faculty meeting.

Over the past three years, I've learned many things about my career and life transition. I thought about what I wished someone had told me when I started taking my first wobbly steps off the academic track. Discover yourself. Cultivate community. Envision what you love.

Here's my practical advice:

Question everything; assume nothing. How do you know if you honestly don't like something until you've tried it? Conversely, do you *know* that you love teaching, or do you just assume that you do because everyone else is gushing about how much they love it? It's okay to admit that you don't love something as much as you thought you did or that you've talked yourself into liking something that isn't a good fit for you. Many academics I know have admitted to me in hushed voices that they hated teaching but pretended to love it. Examine carefully everything that comes into your field of vision. Test-drive some new activities that sound exciting and fun to you. Maybe you volunteer to give tours in a museum or you participate in a service project in your city to help elderly people or you do equine therapy with disabled kids. Maybe you start teaching adult literacy or citizenship classes. Maybe you check out some library books about some new things you've always wanted to pursue and didn't know how. Maybe you start reading about urban farming and find your heart pounding with excitement about helping solve problems of hunger and poverty in your community.

Making mistakes is okay. If you're doing your new nonacademic life right, you're going to make mistakes. Your first steps outside academia probably won't be the right ones at first. Maybe you take a job that doesn't appeal to any of your values or ideas about what's important to you. Maybe you just need a short-term lifeboat job to get some resources together while you're figuring out what you're doing next. Maybe you took a job waiting tables because you need the money but hate it. Maybe you start learning Python and HTML, so you can get a respectable job with a tech company and find that your heart really wants you to be outside working in a park with trees and people. Maybe you enter corporate America and then realize it's sucking your soul dry. Your choices, even if they seem like mistakes, aren't wrong; you're doing research and figuring out what works and what doesn't. Use any and all feedback to make some better choices. It's okay. Learn what you need to and move on to the next thing.

Create a vision. Even if you think your dream is improbable or impractical, it's yours. Your vision is as beautiful, interesting, and unique as you are, and there's no reason that you shouldn't have it. What kind of life do you want to create for yourself? Create the destination and start orienting your choices toward that image. Have faith that the steps will appear when you're ready to take them. You don't need to know everything right now. Sometimes just a little step (or a lurch) in the general direction of your dream is enough. Go as far as you can see; when you get to that point, you'll be able to see a little farther.

Cultivate community. In many fields in the humanities, independent academic achievement remains the gold standard. Sole authorship trumps being the second or third author. Conference papers are best presented as an independent work of a single scholar. In the world outside academia, cultivating community lights the way forward. Cultivate a new network of people outside academia to show you what might be possible. Community makes us stronger and more resilient.

Figure out who can help you reach your new goals and then (and here's the important part) *ask those people for help.* The community you cultivate can help you accomplish the seemingly impossible. Once you figure out where you want to go and what you want to do, the brainpower and connections of your network can help you find a job, meet the right people, find resources, answer questions, create stepping-stones to your dreams, and more. Draw on their expertise and connections. Ask your community for what you need. They want to help you.

You will heal and move forward after leaving academia. Feeling rejected by an institution to which you devoted so much time and money feels devastating. You're heartbroken, which is normal. You'll heal in your own time and on your own schedule. You're going to get through this. Practice lots of self-care. The feelings will probably come in waves because we heal in layers and phases. You can't expect to feel okay in three or four months; the healing process might take years. Meditate on resilience and acceptance. You'll get there.

Stepping off the academic track and into nonacademic life is a process. You don't just decide to leave academia and land the gig of your dreams with a starting salary of $80,000 a year. (Maybe some people do, but I don't know anyone this has actually happened to.) You take little steps toward your big vision, even if you don't know exactly how you're going to get there yet. And those little steps will eventually take you to your dreams.

Finally, as someone who's left academia, you're a talented, creative, re-sourceful, smart, passionate, and persistent person with real skills. Direct your passion toward creating a life that you truly love more than you loved academia. Make a plan for how to get there. Start taking action, one step at a time.

Fly with your new wings.

4

How to Eat an Elephant; or, There's Life outside Academia

RACHEL NEFF

It has been nearly five years since the photo finish in my dissertation, the day before the cutoff to graduate in June. Completing my degree on time was so unlikely that my chair planned his summer research trip, paused, asked himself if he had any students graduating that year, thought "No," and booked his flight abroad for the day before graduation.

Even now, looking back on the past several years since I earned my doctorate in Spanish literature, it would be a lie to say I don't occasionally feel sad about not becoming a professor. That's why I want to start this chapter by asking you, no matter why you're dipping your toes into the alternative-academic job pool, to be kind to yourself. You've spent anywhere from three to eight years surrounded by people who have told you the end goal of this period in your life is to be a professor.

Grief might be part of your transition between the life you dreamed and planned for and the one you are about to embark upon. No timeline exists for when you will feel better about the decision to leave academia. I waffle between anger and fury, relief and rage. Whatever decisions you make about your next steps are the correct ones. No matter if you sever your academic ties immediately or work your way out of academia position by position, the decisions you make after you leave graduate school will be right, because they will be right for you.

Who am I to tell you about this transition? I'm a person who spent my entire academic career striving for perfection. I busted my ass in high school. I constantly beat the odds. I got scholarships and fellowships left and right. In graduate school, I earned my keep—organizing conferences, attending symposiums, serving in student government. I had a 4.0 in high school. I double-majored and double-minored in college. I did everything my professors asked of me in graduate school—and more. Not getting a place at the academic table was a distant concern in my mind. I had always beaten the odds. I thought I might end up in a more rural setting, but having roots in the Midwest, I felt that possibility was more like a homecoming than a problem.

At first, not securing a tenure-track position seemed like failure, one that felt spectacularly public. The grad school grapevine buzzed about professors using me as a cautionary tale and heaping blame on me: how I should have done more summer fellowships, how I should have published papers, and how I shouldn't have followed my (now-ex) partner to another state. The shame burned deep and red across my chest anytime I answered the interviewer's question: "So, why aren't you teaching?"

After a brief and ignoble stint as an adjunct where the pay (after factoring in gas, class prep, and grading) was about $2.50 an hour, I refused to participate in the contingent job market. To be blunt—do not undervalue your labor. Not finding a full-time academic job does not make you any less of a person. You are worthy of a living wage and the dignity of having your work be fairly compensated. The skills and work ethic honed during your advanced studies make you a valuable part of an employer's team. (Or your own team—a lot of folks choose to open their own businesses!) Do not sell yourself short.

When I talk to graduate students about life outside the academy, one of the most shocking things for them to hear is that some jobs pay as much as, if not more than, professorships. For instance, in the United States, many state and federal jobs have pay scales that increase based on the highest level of education obtained. This is why it is important to remember that the best dissertation is a done dissertation.[1] These kinds of pay scales are important research tools when quantifying the value of your labor. Additionally, public-sector jobs often have generous benefits. Take the monetary value of the benefits and add those onto your

---

1. My last chapter was "rough," according to my dissertation director, but it was "good enough to defend." Perfection is the enemy when you are trying to tie up loose ends. Repeat after me: Good is good enough. Also, thank you to Dr. Brian Fox who wrote a really, really long dissertation and defended it the same year as me. By the time my shrimpy 200-page dissertation was ready to defend, my adviser said the length was "just fine." This comment flew in the face of this graduate school conventional wisdom: "Never let anyone defend something under 250 pages."

base salary for private-sector jobs that do not have equally robust benefits packages. Never, ever doubt what an employer will pay for an intelligent and dedicated worker. The most difficult part to explain to your future employer (or client, if you go the freelance route) is how your skillset matches their company needs.

How do you go about finding that first job after graduate school? Before I answer that, I want to share a riddle with you: How do you eat an elephant? Answer: One bite at a time. This advice got me through graduate school. The job search is a giant elephant, and you're going to tackle the big, scary beast one bite at a time.

Now, I come from a position of privilege—my parents could help me financially, and my partner at the time was able to support both of us as I searched for work. While I recognize my privilege made the transition to the alternative-academic (alt-ac), and then nonacademic, work world much easier, many of the key takeaways from my job searches are applicable to those looking to transition to more stable employment. My approach to post-academic life is as follows:

- assess your skills and identify potential industries where you could thrive
- network with everyone and let your network know you're looking for work
- read job ads and absorb the lingo to replicate/mimic that language in your application
- focus on three job-related tasks per week.

Shortly, I'll break down those actions into more manageable chunks to clarify your next steps.

That's not to say this process is easy. I'm not some poster child for a happy life outside academia. I still read through job ads and deeply wish my turn on the academic market had resulted in interviews and a job. I bought the Wonka bar. I thought it had my Golden Ticket. Reflecting on my dissertation year and the nine-month search for employment, I still have regrets and second thoughts. For most graduate students, the course of study leads to one conclusion: teaching and/or researching. Thus, when you leave the academy and don't follow the set path, the future can feel impossible. Bleak, even. You might turn to academic mentors who have never searched for work outside academia. However, that's not to say those mentors don't have connections. While they might not be able to help you prep for a foray into the sexist viper pit that is Silicon

Valley, their uncle's cousin's friend might be able to get you a second look at a job.

Don't feel as though an alternative academic career is a consolation prize. Treat the job search outside the academy with as much intensity and fervor as you treated your academic one. This means tailoring cover letters, updating résumés, and presenting yourself in a way that fits your chosen industry. However, do not—do *not*—bid too low. Don't take a job that is so below your skill set that you feel bored or unhappy with your work. Unlike academia, the eight-to-five world is really miserable very quickly if you are doing something you dislike. Think of everything you learned (or didn't) about preparing for the academic job market. The CVs. The sample syllabi. The statement of teaching philosophy. You aren't going to use many (if any) of those materials. Buckle up. It's time to get down to the nitty-gritty.

Figure out what to do once you decide not to try for (or continue on) the academic track. This is the most overwhelming step of the process. Instead of applying to every job that might possibly fit your interests, you are going to take a step back and assess what end result you want to achieve. There are many ways to approach your alt-ac job search. If you need to secure employment as soon as possible after graduation, then here's the plan of attack: (1) inventory your skills, (2) determine any economic or geographic restrictions to your preferred job path, and (3) decide what salary range you want to accept. The rest are details.

Let's break down the plan of attack a bit more. For many graduate students, translating the skills acquired during their studies is difficult. How do you explain the reading, writing, and critical thinking to a lay audience? A lot of employers know a PhD means you are smart. That doesn't mean they understand how you, in your round peg–ness, will fit into their square hole. Start making a list of all the things you did during your studies. Reading multiple books and articles per week? Serving on committees? Organizing conferences? Making presentations?

Even though you will most likely limit or minimize mention of those activities on your résumé, they formed an important foundation you can build on at a company. Those research skills, your attention to detail, and the ability to review and weigh evidence can be unclear to most employers. You have to translate your skills into their language. Not every employer is as excited about (or even cares about) your main subject matter expertise. In several cover letters, I would explicitly call out what my ability to read a lot on a tight schedule meant for them. I said, "I am able to read and synthesize a large volume of text in a short amount of time, while also weighing the validity and importance of the information presented." Instead of saying, "I read a lot of books and articles," I made my skills tangible and useful for my future employer.

You have to build the brand of you, so you can explain how your skills fit the needs of your future employer. Their biggest concerns will be that you are overqualified and that you will go back to teaching the first chance you get. Have calm, thoughtful responses to their concerns. If someone says they think you might be overqualified, let them know what exactly about the job appeals to you. I once said in an interview that the hardest part of the job (that required using Associated Press style) would be giving up the Oxford comma, but that I was so excited about the job that I was willing to give it up. For those who are afraid you're going to teach the minute you're given the chance, you have to reassure them that you have a five-year plan for the new industry you want to break into.

Don't make your future employer guess how you'll fit into the company. The cover letter is a great place to explain how your background and talent fit the employer's needs. (If you get into marketing, we call this their pain points.) You are there to fix and solve problems. I told one interviewer to think of me as the future office MacGyver—ready, willing, and able to solve whatever task they threw my way. Based on the job description, I could tell that the employer was looking for someone who could wear many hats and turn around projects on tight deadlines. Every answer I gave in the interview was geared toward showcasing my ability to juggle multiple, demanding projects while still producing quality work.

How do you learn the language of employers when very few (if any) people around you have experience outside academia? That's where the next steps come along.

To learn the language of the employer, you will have to do research. I know, after slogging through a doctoral program, that the idea of more research isn't appealing. In fact, the idea of searching for something other than what you've trained for is overwhelming. Many, many jobs that would be a good fit are out there. The result is that everything feels out of reach and out of control. What do you need to do?

Focus on three things each day that move the job search forward. I'm not talking three lofty things. The three things may be as simple as getting dressed, making food, and looking at one job posting. Again, searching for a job outside academia can take months. Landing a full-time job took me nine months. Pace yourself. While it is important to apply to jobs on the earlier side of the listing, you also will learn valuable things during each job application.

Narrow your weekly scope to one kind of job opening. Here's my key to cracking the code: Look at positions in places and at companies you wouldn't necessarily want to move to or work for. Research by area. Learn the lingo. You have to speak to the correct audience. Translate your skills and knowledge in a way that explains how you will meet your future employer's needs. Let's break it down:

- Conference presentations? → You can deliver client reports.
- Group projects for seminars? → You can work in a team to create quality deliverables.
- Major research projects? → You have project management skills.
- All that reading for classes and exams? → You can read large amounts of text and synthesize complex information.
- All the papers you wrote? → You have exceptional writing skills that show your ability to review and weigh evidence.
- Teaching? → You can manage a room of thirty people for one to three hours. It's called classroom management for a reason.

Look at the job descriptions to see the language these companies use to talk about their expectations for the position. By doing so, you will acquire a new way to describe your skills: on-time deliverables, project management experience, ability to complete job duties with minimal supervision, and so on.

As a lifelong *Star Wars* fan, I like to paraphrase Han Solo's "Keep your distance . . . but don't look like you're keeping your distance" line as "Imitate the job ad, but don't make it look like you're imitating the job ad. Apply casual." Take enough phrases and verbiage to illustrate how your skills fit the employer's needs and then add a few things of your own.

However, a résumé is not a CV. Please: edit, edit, edit. Search for sample résumés in the field that interests you. Most should be no longer than two pages, preferably one. If you want to pass for a duck, you gotta learn how to quack.

How do you add your own twist to what a job posting asks for? That's where your crackerjack research skills come into play. Look at other, similar jobs and see what those folks are looking for. That is why you will focus your energy each week on one type of job (a vertical, if you will). That's not to say you should ignore a great job that might pop up on your radar that week if it's not within the vertical. It's more to say that when you're feeling overwhelmed, you can channel your energy and enthusiasm into a more narrow range of options. You have to keep moving forward. But baby steps. Baby duckling steps. As with picking a dissertation or thesis topic, selecting what type of job you want to pursue in your alt-ac or post-ac life can seem daunting.

What kind of jobs should you apply for? If anyone has mentioned a position you'd be perfect for, start there. Look at job titles. Then, envision what you want to do. Do you want or need to stay in a particular geographic region? What is most important to you in a career? Prestige? Salary? Flexibility? Next, approach potential employment from a place of admiration. Is there a company you love? Call and ask if you could get a tour or spend half a day shadowing folks at the business. Is there a person within the profession or industry you admire? Ask for an informational interview or a coffee meeting to learn more about the field or industry. I learned these tips after I had started in the marketing industry. I helped arrange informational coffee interviews and half-day tours of the business I worked for. Those folks gained a lot of information and soaked up the employees' knowledge of the day-to-day routine. Go-sees and interviews aren't just for college students. Many individuals who branch out on their own or are looking to make a career change take advantage of these activities to decide who their ideal clients might be or to see if the field is a good fit for them.

Otherwise, take a job or skills fit test. Yes, I've heard the joke that these tests are the new horoscopes for millennials. Nevertheless, assessments are very helpful in guiding you through the next steps in your life. No one test has all the answers, but taking a few free online tests (or a book test from something at your local library or school's career center) might help spark some ideas of what futures are possible. Moreover, by categorizing and cataloging your strengths and weaknesses, you will better understand what aspects of nonacademic work you might find interesting. (And what areas or types of work you would be better off avoiding.)

If you feel as though you don't know where to start, even after taking a skills test, consider using your campus or city's career services. Perhaps consider using a recruiter to help place you. (Note: You should not pay a recruiter up front. The company pays the recruiter when you are hired.) Remember to update social media. If you don't have a professional social media profile, make one. In the private sector, many employers look at prospects' profiles on sites such as LinkedIn as part of the hiring process. While this advice may bring back memories of researching careers in middle and high school, it's not that far off. You're restarting the career path you thought you would take. I grieved. In some ways, I still grieve the dream I stopped pursuing because I knew my labor was worth more.

Remember, you are not alone in the job search. Maybe your academic experience has left you hesitant to ask others for help, but outside academia, people are looking to connect. I know academic life is about making it on your own and blazing your own trail. That's great for some things. But for finding a nonacademic job, hunkering down and keeping to yourself is a recipe for disaster.

Here's the number one rule for job search success: You never know what place might need an employee like you, so let everyone know you're on the market. Everyone. My car insurance agent offered to put me in touch with his wife who was a principal at a school district needing bilingual teachers and willing to sponsor emergency teaching licenses. How did I find this out? I told him I was looking for work while filling out my insurance paperwork.

Put your social network on alert. Call. Email. Text. Let them know what you're looking for and how best to tell you about opportunities. Within the academy, networking is made harder by academic egos. Outside academia, networking is lifeblood. There's a popular adage that an estimated 70 percent of jobs in the private sector aren't advertised, but rather found by word of mouth. Real example: I went to a friend's show at a bar. We got to chatting. He mentioned his workplace was going to double the team size. My stand partner at orchestra has a kid who trained in that same industry. The kid was having trouble landing that first job after college. I realized that my friend's company and my stand partner's kid might be a good match. I put them in touch. Where was this job advertised? Nowhere else. These types of situations happen all the time—even before a job listing is written.

Tell people in casual conversation you are looking for work. Look for meetups in areas of interest. Use the alumni network of every place you've gone to school. Networking is about finding common points of interest and helping each other through the world. Most schools have alumni in almost every state. Where did you graduate from? Is there a sporting event or meetup scheduled near you? These are people who might be able to introduce you to your next job. While I've never used my alumni network this way, I do know of other folks who have and ended up with strong mentors who helped guide and shape their careers. To that end, keep in mind that the people you initially reach out to might not be able to help you, but they might offer to make introductions to their network. Also, maybe the person you tell that you're looking for work will find a job you passed over and say it's perfect for you. It's very helpful to have someone else say, "No, you should go for that job."

One of the hardest parts for me after a job search that resulted in zero interviews was shaking off the feeling of failure. The most important thing to do at this stage is to reframe the narrative from "I've failed" to "What's next?" Framing your nonacademic job search as another step, as something that is moving you forward, helps the transition away from academia. Hearing other people echo that certain jobs would be a good fit for me boosted my confidence. Outside academia, people quit things all the time. People change jobs. Change careers. Moving around and changing one's mind are commonplace. Quitting academia is not some scarlet letter outside academia. This is how the conversation typically goes:

- "Why aren't you teaching?"
- "Each year, there are fewer and fewer tenure-track positions in my field, and I wanted to bring my skills and knowledge to the admin side/nonprofit world/private sector."
- "What are you doing now?"

There is no scandal if you leave the academy. Remember, be gentle with yourself. The world outside academia is far more collaborative and compassionate than your experience in graduate school might have you believe.

Each time you apply for a job, ask your social network if anyone knows someone who works at that company. Sometimes it's a long shot. But, I have personally witnessed job candidates who were initially put in a "no" pile be reconsidered because someone sent an email or made a call on their behalf. I've also gotten a job interview because someone I met at a house party made an introduction on my behalf. All because I mentioned I had applied to the company and hadn't heard back. Within a day of the introduction, I was called for an interview. It doesn't hurt to ask if your network knows someone where you're applying. Don't discount the positive impact a good word on your behalf can have on your job search.

If all goes well, you will be invited to interview. Indeed, getting a job interview is the hardest part. Interviews for nonacademic jobs are not like those for academic jobs. If you listen to one piece of advice, listen to this: a nonacademic job interview is not an academic job talk. Don't talk yourself out of the job. A job interview is not a confession or a gripe session. Be prepared to succinctly (think 140 characters or less) explain the topic of your thesis. Although the book is out of print and some of the questions are dated, Robert Half's *The Robert Half Way to Get Hired* is a helpful resource.[2] In the interview, be prepared to explain any gaps in your work history. The interview is a game of getting you to reveal too much. Here are the top five questions I remember being asked during my interviews:

- Would you go back to teaching?
- Tell me about a time you had a conflict with a coworker. What happened, and how did you resolve it?
- Have you ever missed a deadline?
- Tell me about a time you worked on a team. What was your role, and how did the group function?
- Why are you interested in this job?

As part of the interview, it's important to have good follow-up questions. Some of my favorites are:

- Can you describe a typical day in this role?
- What are the opportunities for growth?
- What are the biggest challenges facing this role?
- What are the expectations for success in the first ninety days at this company?
- What are the next steps in the interview process, and when can I expect to hear from you about them?

During the interview, you want to show skills, competence, and a positive attitude. A job interview is not a venting session. Perhaps this is why I ended up working in public relations for two years, but the ability to put a positive spin on things makes it much easier to hire you. An employer needs to be convinced you want to be there and that you aren't going to bolt the first chance you get. A firm and polite "I am leaving the academy to explore new opportunities and use my skills in the private / nonprofit sector" or "I've always enjoyed [subject] and this job was a perfect fit" are sufficient answers to any probing questions. Again, do not treat the job interview like

2. I am grateful to Dr. Diana Dodson Lee for her assistance preparing me for my first alternative-academic interview. She took me through many of the questions in this book and coached me on ways to improve my answers. Her real-world experience outside the academy was incredibly helpful and made future interviews much easier.

a job talk. A nonacademic boss is not your colleague. You are going to be hired to fulfill a need and perform a role.

Be warned, though, that employers might lie to you during the job interview process. I quit a job when I realized the opportunities for growth within the department were greatly exaggerated. During the interview, I asked what the opportunities for advancement would look like. When a role above me opened up, they used an outside job placement agency rather than hiring internally. I realized then and there that I would never be advanced in the organization and that they would always look for talent from outside for upper management positions. Once that happened, I started looking elsewhere and moved on.

Another important lesson I learned was to negotiate your salary and benefits. Don't accept an offer if it feels lowball. Use online resources to find the typical salary for similar job titles in the region. Make sure you aren't taking on the lion's share of work for poor recompense. Feeling undervalued is a surefire way to start resenting a job and have you looking for another one in short order.

Also, you don't have to take the first job you are offered. If it doesn't feel like the right fit, you can decline. In the working world, I've seen several employees come through who work for a week or two and then quit. Coming from academia where it seems everyone is there forever, it was shocking. But in the private sector, a lot of people move on quickly.

That's how you eat the elephant of the job hunt. You break it into smaller parts and focus on a few things at a time. Reframe your mind-set from "I'm a failure" to "I'm doing what is best for me and figuring out what comes next." Me? I work eight-to-five in a job that has nothing to do with my PhD or MFA. I go home and run my freelance editing and writing business. I work on publishing my creative writing. I knit. I watch TV. I plan out a book tour for my poetry chapbook, *The Haywire Heart and Other Musings on Love*. Sure, I look at teaching jobs every now and then, but I've put down roots. I bought a home near family. I am happy with the place I landed in life. I don't want or need to chase the academic dream any more. I'm complete as a person with a doctorate who isn't a tenure-track professor. It doesn't hurt that I'm earning as much as many assistant professors do.

Yes, I miss the flexibility with my work schedule, but I do enjoy my job. The hardest part is right after you leave. It is a difficult period of time. I have come out the other side, and you will too. I promise. Forgive yourself for not wanting to let go of the person you thought you would become. Instead, embrace the person you want to become next. Three small things a day will get you there. Now, go on, get quacking.

5

Run toward Yourself

CATHY HANNABACH

As my friends can attest, I am a big fan of *The West Wing*, a television show that ran from 1999 to 2006 on NBC (and is now getting some renewed attention thanks to the fabulous West Wing Weekly podcast). In one episode, "Swiss Diplomacy," President Jed Bartlet is giving advice to Sam Seaborn, the deputy communications director who, due to a strange confluence of events, is now running for Congress. The president tells Sam that when he needs to, Sam should feel free to "run away" from the president. When Sam objects, thinking he is being advised to sell out his beloved boss for cheap political points, President Bartlet interjects: "I appreciate that, but that's not what I meant." And then the president tells Sam something that I am going to offer as advice for building a career beyond academia: "Run toward yourself. I'm wrong about that. Walk. You're not going to be used to your surroundings."

This is the story of how I ran, walked, and danced toward myself as I moved from college professor to founder and president of Ideas on Fire. In the process, I discovered that building a life and a world beyond the academy means using your whole self.

My Journey

I went to college at the University of California at Berkeley, intending to be a feminist journalist and continue my dancing as an unrelated artistic practice. Two weeks into my first semester, I discovered women's and gender studies as a field. I switched my major and spent the next four years organizing conferences and teach-ins, running activist organizations, turning my love of dance into multimedia performance nights, planning rallies and poetry readings, and teaching community education courses. I reveled in the fact that for the first time in my life I was surrounded by people who combined social justice activism, creativity, performance, and voracious intellectual inquiry—and somehow built a career out of it.

Early in my undergrad years I attended graduate student events and took graduate seminars, learning everything I could about academia as an industry because I was enthralled. I was lucky to have professors and mentors who were willing to teach me about things like tenure clocks and departmental structure (I suspect they were mostly amused that an eighteen-year-old would care). I sat on two faculty hiring committees in my capacity as president of the Women's Studies Student Association, which opened my eyes about the hiring process from the department side, and I watched several graduate students and contingent faculty navigate the academic job market, which showed me the applicant side.

I remember clearly the week my mentor Gayle Salamon gave me a copy of Marc Bousquet's article "The Waste Product of Graduate Education: Toward a Dictatorship of the Flexible," as she saw I was itching to go to grad school and dreaming of the professorial life.[1] She didn't want to discourage me but did want me to go into it with eyes wide open, knowing to expect many years on the job market and in contingent faculty positions, with little hope of landing a tenure-track gig. This was 2002, long before the 2008 global economic crash (there never really were those alleged "good ol' days" of the academic job market). I read the article, fascinated, and we talked a lot about it over the next few years as I watched her piece together contingent positions and apply yearly to tenure-track jobs.

I voraciously dove into academia as an industry while an undergraduate—I learned which journals "counted" in my fields and why, submitted my first article for publication to GLQ (it was rejected, but the learning process was invaluable), presented at conferences, and wrote two bachelor of arts theses requiring me to travel for research. For four years, I also co-taught a hybrid academic / community education course on sexual and domestic violence prevention, during which I designed a curriculum that enabled me to learn new skills while teaching, to lead discussions and manage group conflict, to translate between diverse stakeholders such as community organizations and university departments, to break down complex ideas into their component parts, and to build professional com-

1. Marc Bousquet, "The Waste Product of Graduate Education: Toward a Dictatorship of the Flexible," *Social Text* 20, no. 1 (2002): 81–104.

munity through teaching people's work and letting the creators know about it.

Like a lot of college students, I had a variety of jobs, including serving as the program coordinator for the Gender Equity Resource Center, which entailed organizing dozens of events each year, ranging from feminist financial independence workshops and racial justice speaker panels to queer mixers, disability rights film screenings, and trans* art shows. I also did freelance editing work for professors and fellow students. And finally, I was a personal care attendant for a fellow student, Alex, who had cerebral palsy. In that job, I was a mixture of health care worker, writing coach, tutor, note taker, editor, and disability advocate, which taught me a lot about state disability services as well as contingent labor organizing. At the time, disability health care workers in California like myself were quasi-unionized through the Service Employees International Union but were still contingent labor who had no long-term contracts or benefits. I had no idea how relevant those lessons would be to my professorial career.

I went straight to graduate school after getting my BA in 2005, which I tell students is generally a terrible idea but in my case was the right one. I did my PhD in cultural studies at the University of California at Davis, focusing on queer studies and visual culture, and wrote a dissertation about queer corporeal ethics in art and performance. During graduate school I continued doing the kind of activist and community arts work I had done throughout my undergraduate years, interweaving it into my scholarship and teaching: organizing conferences, founding and leading student groups, writing pieces about artists with whom I had worked, and accepting journal article review requests to learn about the academic publishing industry.

For income during graduate school (2005–2010), I taught courses and took research assistant positions. I noticed that professors would request me as their research assistant after hearing about me from their colleagues, and I spun that into a steady slew of those positions. I further honed skills that I had developed in activist and arts organizations and my freelance work: project management, organization and scheduling, team building and management, accounting, developmental editing and copyediting, building digital databases, and keeping abreast of industry trends and best practices to advise on projects. I developed a real knack for helping people get from "I have an awesome idea!" to a concrete action plan with deadlines that reflected their real-life resources, time, and energy levels. In 2009, I also turned my haphazard freelancing into a side business, one that several years later I would rename Ideas on Fire.

When I finished my PhD in 2010, I picked up and moved across the country to take a one-year, possibly renewable contingent faculty position at the University of Pittsburgh. During my two years in Pittsburgh, I continued my academic editing and indexing business. Because I had only five to ten hours per week to devote to it, it brought in only a few thousand dollars a year, but that was enough to pay for me to go to conferences in the desperate hope I could find a tenure-track job.

During my Pittsburgh years (2010–2012), I got serious about my side business. I took on more clients and honed my editing and indexing skills on diverse client projects. I invested in specialized software and a real invoicing system. I took tons of online courses on editing, indexing, and business models. At academic conferences, I set up informational interviews with acquisitions editors and publishing executives to learn about their daily lives on the job. I also mapped out the networks of developmental editors, indexers, packagers, editorial assistants, and acquisitions editors that authors thanked in their acknowledgments sections—this was a map of the industry I was slowly becoming more and more a part of. And most importantly, I started publicly identifying as a professional editor and indexer, making it easier for clients to find and hire me.

In 2012 my contingent faculty contract ran out, so when my wife Adrienne got a tenure-track job in Philadelphia, we moved again. I taught as an adjunct at Temple University and the University of Pennsylvania for two years. I also ran my academic editing and indexing business on the side, which by that point had grown so much I was consistently having to turn down clients because I didn't have the time to take them on while teaching full-time.

In Philadelphia, I kept doing my community arts and activist work, using it as a way to meet people in a new city, develop professional skills and networks, and fulfill my desire to share more social justice–oriented art and culture. I joined the board of DP Arts (a performance arts nonprofit), volunteered with Phreak N' Queer (a local music festival), and founded Philly Queer Media (a community arts organization), which I ran for two years. For those looking to explore careers in the arts, joining local arts organizations and organizing events with them can be a great way to get your foot in the door. It also lets you connect with impressive artists, dancers, oral historians, radical archivists, filmmakers, community television producers, and DJs.

I started attending local meetings of Versatile PhD, a supportive organization that helps people with PhDs craft careers beyond the academy. Talking with faculty and graduate students who were considering leaving academia, as well as people who had done so long ago and now had fulfilling careers elsewhere, showed me I had options. Additionally, the vibrant and vocal alternative-academic/post-academic (alt-ac/post-ac) community I found on Twitter was invaluable.

The nationwide network of artists, activists, cultural workers, nonprofit directors, performers, and community organizers I had built over the years provided role models for the alt-ac life. Many of them have advanced degrees or maintain diverse relationships to academia. Though not the case for the traditional disciplines, the social justice–oriented interdisciplines like women's studies, ethnic studies, queer studies, and disability studies always built these networks. For those of us who trained in those fields, meshing art, activism, and academia is natural. Although leaving academia was devastating—as it is for most people in terms of having to give up the hard-won professorial identity—I was able to build a life and a career beyond it because of my experience with brilliant, creative people who had intellectually and politically fulfilling lives elsewhere. I can't overemphasize how valuable role models are in this sense.

By the summer of 2013, I had been on the job market for four years and was staring down a fifth one. I had spent more than $10,000 on my multiyear academic job search, and at that point I just couldn't bear the emotional or financial cost of another that I knew wouldn't yield anything. I knew it was time to go.

I used my last semester of teaching as an adjunct to further explore career options. I researched and applied for jobs in grant writing, community arts management, nonprofits, curriculum development, and publishing. I also thought hard about what to do with the business I had built and run since 2009. Ultimately, I decided to try to turn my business into a full-time job. At that point, it had never brought in enough revenue to support me. But I decided to try, and I was privileged enough to have a partner who could cover more of our living expenses.[2] I taught my last class as a professor in December 2013 and said goodbye to the professorial dream, ready for a new year and a new life.

In the first four months of running my company full-time, I blew

---

2. I realize this is not possible for everyone and this economic privilege needs to be made clear. Starting a full-time business, even one you've been running part-time for many years as I had, is an incredibly risky financial move. But given that I was making $14,000 a year as an adjunct (less than I made as a graduate student), I figured I didn't have a lot to lose. I decided to give it six months and if it couldn't support me, I'd go back to applying for jobs at nonprofits, publishing houses, and community arts organizations.

through my meager savings paying credit card bills and student loans, while my wife generously covered a lot of our living expenses. But the business took off. I could take on the clients I previously had to turn down due to time constraints, and I could develop new offers based on client feedback. I continued participating in professional editing and publishing associations and taking (mostly free) courses on editing and indexing, business models, digital marketing strategy, company infrastructure, hiring, and team management.

I started hiring people part-time when I could afford it and have now built an amazing team that helps progressive, interdisciplinary thinkers write and publish work, enliven public conversations, and create more just worlds. It has been a wild ride, and I have loved it. Running a company, especially one employing other people (even part-time), is incredibly hard. But I have always adored projects that push me to learn a ton of new things and grow in the process. Running Ideas on Fire fits the bill. I have never had so much fun. I get to be more "me" in running Ideas on Fire than I ever did in the academy, where my community arts and activist work didn't count for much on the job market or in promotion requirements (even though individual colleagues and department chairs supported it).

Making the Transition

So if you're a current or former academic considering a career beyond the academy, what advice would I have? Like the president tells Sam on *The West Wing*, I advise you to run (or walk, skip, or twirl) toward yourself. Look back over the varied projects you've done over your life—what are the common threads that bind those varied things together? Those threads are *you*, they tie together even tangential things you did, and they're what you usually have to excise from or downplay on your CV when you apply for faculty jobs. That's the "you" I recommend you run toward, even as that you is changing. So how do you do that?

Create Projects to Learn Skills

As much post-ac/alt-ac advice emphasizes, beyond the academy you are evaluated much more on your skills than on your knowledge. One concrete way to see this is in language: academic CVs use nouns (research/teaching areas: queer studies, visual culture, phenomenology), whereas résumés use verbs (researched and tested SEO best practices for feminist blog posts, designed and implemented a social media campaign resulting in X number of new followers/engagements, solicited and edited submissions from X number of authors). This is not to say that knowledge is unimportant or you won't use it in your career beyond the academy. But you need to start thinking about your experience and background in terms of what you can do.

One way to make this shift is to design each project you work on—from your dissertation to your academic service work and classroom teaching—to teach you a specific set of skills. Let's say you are curious about a possible communications or marketing career where you get to translate ideas across diverse audiences. You might consider starting a blog about one of your dissertation chapter topics. Treat the time and labor you spend training yourself in website platforms, blogging norms, voice and tone, editing, and social media marketing as part of your dissertation project. Those practices will not only help you work through the critical analysis necessary to produce your scholarly argument, but also enable you to develop concrete skills that are relevant beyond the academy.

Or if, as I was, you're curious about how arts nonprofits work and whether you'd do well in that industry, see if you can team up with a local nonprofit to organize a conference on your campus. Take the time to talk to the nonprofit's staff and observe how they spend their days. You can ask for informational interviews with your new colleagues and have a much better chance of getting them because you've already been working together.

How about teaching? You can use the classroom as a chance to develop concrete skills applicable beyond academia. Think about creative assignments you can design for students that give you the chance to not only learn new tools and practices but also teach them to others. For example, design an assignment in which you have students create a podcast episode to accompany a critical essay. If you've never done that before, then you have given yourself the opportunity to research podcasting practices, show development, genre conventions and the different time and resource commitments they require, audio editing tools and best practices, recording equipment, audio storytelling techniques, hosting platforms, and podcast publishing. It's also an opportunity to learn how to teach these tools and skills to others. You'll discover the clearest way to present this information, how much tinkering time people need to figure out audio editing software, and the financial, technological, and corporeal barriers to using various tools.

Get Comfortable Talking about Money

Money is one of those things that makes many people squirm. Most undergrads, grad students, and contingent faculty tend not to have much of it, so the thought of financial planning seems like a cruel joke. If you grew up in a context in which someone else dealt with the household finances, you might not have much direct knowledge of salaries, budgeting, interest rates, or saving for retirement. And goodness knows academia does everything possible to prevent its workers (i.e., faculty and graduate students) from valuing their labor in terms of money, which is why it feels so hard to negotiate for a higher salary, unionize, or calculate your hourly wage. But the time to get over that fear of money is now—it's a process, I know, but you can start now.

My friend Kate Drabinski, who has been one of my alt-ac/post-ac role models since I met her during my first women's studies course in college, likes to remind me that "there is no clean living under capitalism." She means that there is no pure, 100 percent righteous way to exist in the world under systems of oppression. Our lives and careers are tainted from the get-go. But that doesn't mean we throw up our hands and say anything goes. It doesn't mean we stick our heads in the sand and pretend our work within and beyond the academy is purely "a calling" or detached from global capital and its violence. It also doesn't mean we stop valuing our labor and the labor of others. It's crucial that we do quite the opposite.

As feminist, economic justice, and racial justice activists have pointed out since the invention of capitalism (and earlier), not talking about money harms marginalized people. Pretending that money isn't important, is too confusing, or is somehow beneath you and the "life of the mind" is a damn nifty ideological trick that white supremacist heteropatriarchy loves. Don't fall for it. Figure out what you're worth and demand it. Yes, it feels weird. Yes, you will probably cringe the first few times (or few dozen times) you give a price quote to a client, ask your boss for a raise, demand payment for an unpaid invoice, or send an organization your speaking fee. Do it anyway.

For people with PhDs first exploring jobs beyond the academy, this can be particularly difficult because, on the one hand, you have a lot of (expensive) education, but on the other hand, you lack the direct work experience that commands higher wages. Remember that having a PhD doesn't mean you deserve the same salary as someone who has been working in a particular industry for five years or more, but it also doesn't mean you are stuck making minimum wage forever. Use informational interviews to learn as much as you can about salaries and hourly rates in the industries that intrigue you. Put your research chops to work comparing salaries across geographic locations and years on the job. Knowing that concrete skills are worth more than knowledge outside the academy, you can develop those skills that make you marketable in the fields you're pursuing and give you the confidence to get more comfortable talking about compensation.

Build (New) Community

Leaving academia requires you to make new friends and find new mentors. That doesn't mean you lose the important ones you found in the academy. But to truly understand the vast array of options and lives beyond the professoriate, you need to spend time with people who are not in it. Dissertation directors can be invaluable as you navigate academic life. But unless they have worked extensively and recently in a career beyond the academy, they are not the best mentors for building a nonacademic career. Similarly, if all your friends are academics, you have limited opportunities to see examples of fulfilling lives beyond academia.

Try hanging out with people you never would have thought of before; join community groups or organizations in your area. Try to find groups that are interested in things you like, whether those are sports, dance, art, gardening, cooking, woodworking, or theater. Coworking communities can also be a great way to meet diverse people from varied careers. For example, when I left academia I joined Indy Hall, a coworking community in Philadelphia. Through Indy Hall I've met a bunch of folks. Some come from fields I knew, like publishing, community arts, activism, performance, and education. Even better, others come from fields I had little-to-no experience with, like computer programming, digital marketing, government policy, cookbook writing, and app development. I've been able to adapt strategies and practices I learned from them to my own company and industry.

Try Lots of Stuff—Fail at It, Learn from It, Try More

One of the most important things you'll learn when transitioning out of the academy can also be the most challenging, and that's what you want to do with your life, at least right now. When I left academia, I declared my first year out as my year of "yes" (this was before Shonda Rhimes's book of the same name came out, but it's a similar principle).[3] That meant that when an opportunity presented itself, unless I truly did not want to do it or couldn't, I said yes. New person from my coworking space invites me to lunch? Yes, to talk to someone I otherwise would never have met and try a

3. Shonda Rhimes, *Year of Yes: How to Dance It Out, Stand in Your Sun, and Be Your Own Person* (New York: Simon and Schuster, 2016).

new lunch spot. Publisher asks me if I could try my hand at editing short stories? Yes, to learn if I could add fiction editing to my nonfiction editing services. Friend asks if I could review her grant application for a community oral history project? Yes, to discern if I wanted to apply for grant-writing jobs. Sign up for a free class on starting a nonprofit? Yes, to decide whether I could turn Philly Queer Media into a nonprofit (I decided against it). Offer to design a website for a filmmaker friend? Yes, to find out if I wanted to design websites for artists and activist organizations as a career. Become the treasurer for DP Arts? Yes, to put my previous accounting experience to work in a community arts context and see if that could be a potential career path.

When deciding what to try, figure out how many free labor hours you can dedicate to learning and how many of those hours need to be paid so you can cover your living expenses. Seek out paid learning opportunities when possible, but also think broadly about compensation—time, resources, and advice also count (after all, those are things you'd pay money for anyway). If you want to develop your editing skills on someone's article but they can't afford to pay you, could you trade a copyedit for résumé advice or them cooking you a meal? If the only positions available with a local organization are volunteer spots, can you use that to also meet potential grant-writing clients? If your first job out of academia is not where you want to end up (which will probably be the case), what concrete skills and networks can you develop there that can make you more competitive for other jobs? In the examples above, some of those "yes" practices were paid in money and the others were paid in either barter or concrete skill development that cost less than a course on the same topic.

Figure Out What You Like—and What You Don't

One of the most exciting parts of any career change is the opportunity to figure out what you really like and don't like. When we're in the daily grind of a job, we don't usually ask this question because we're too busy with obligations.

When figuring out what career(s) you might want to build beyond the academy, I recommend *not* starting with industries. The question "Which industries could I see myself in beyond academia?" is not useful for folks who have had very few encounters with other industries. Most academics' knowledge of industries is pretty limited to higher education and some of the academic-adjacent industries like scholarly publishing (a small part of the larger publishing industry), academic editing (a small part of the larger editing industry), and K–12 education.

The typical graduate will be stuck with an unhelpfully myopic set of options. After all, you can't picture yourself as something you've never seen. Instead, I recommend you figure out how you enjoy spending your days. What environments, practices, relationships, and communication styles make you happy, expansive, and brilliant? Which shut you down? Think with your whole body here—we're bodies in the world before and after we're anything else.

Once you've figured this out, read job ads and do informational interviews (remember that new community you built?) to find jobs that let you do those things most days.

How to Run toward Yourself When That Self Is Changing

A year into running Ideas on Fire full-time, I started a podcast called Imagine Otherwise in which I get to interview artists, activists, and academics who bridge those three realms in the service of social justice. The array of talent, creativity, and brilliance these folks embody is dizzying, and I feel privileged to create a platform for their work. But my favorite part of hosting Imagine Otherwise is an interview question I ask each guest, one that gets at the heart of the podcast, Ideas on Fire, my career within and beyond academia, and really everything I've ever done: What kind of world are you working toward? What kind of world do you want?

Most guests, particularly in the early days of the podcast when nobody had listened to past episodes, giggled nervously at first and said something like, "Oh, I don't know if I'm the best person to answer this. It's such a big question." And it is. It's huge. But it is one we don't ask each other enough and one we don't have enough opportunities to answer for ourselves. It's also the question that can help you run toward yourself, even when that self is changing.

I discovered the power of this question several years ago when teaching Amber Hollibaugh's book *My Dangerous Desires: A Queer Girl Dreaming Her Way Home* in a women's studies course. In the foreword, queer southern novelist Dorothy Allison recalls the first conversation the two had in a coffee shop, the one that confirmed that this would be a power femme friendship for life. Allison writes, "Revolutions begin when people look each other in the eyes, say 'I want,' and mean it. We meant it."[4] I asked my students what they wanted, what they really wanted. At first, I got nervous

4. Dorothy Allison, "Foreword," in Amber Hollibaugh, *My Dangerous Desires: A Queer Girl Dreaming Her Way Home* (Durham, NC: Duke University Press, 2000), xiii.

giggling and brush-offs. Some made jokes about wanting a good grade in the class. I waited. And the outpouring came—the students wanted to build different worlds and use their whole selves in doing it, they wanted to not cordon off pieces of themselves in the process. But most significantly, most of them told me they had never been asked before. My podcast guests, many of whom are senior scholars or world-renowned artists and activists, echo this—they've never been asked.

So what do you really want? What kind of world do you want, and how do you want to help build it? That's the self you run toward, the self you walk toward, the self you dance toward and with.

6

What Would Your Poor Husband Do?
Living with the Two-Body Problem

KELLY J. BAKER

In the fall of 2008, I had a campus interview for a tenure-track position in the religious studies department of a flagship state university. It was one of three campus visits I had that fall. My adviser told
me that I was sure to get a tenure-track job because I was a stellar
candidate. My dissertation was under review by an academic press.
My CV included conference presentations, articles, book reviews,
and an award for creativity in research. I had already created and
taught a number of classes. I accomplished all these things before
I even graduated with my PhD. Yet, I was nervous about my job
search. My daughter had been born before conference season in religious studies, so I had phone interviews rather than the standard
conference interviews. I took calls with search committees while
my newborn slept and my mother-in-law watched her.

I became a mother and a PhD almost simultaneously.

The campus visit seemed to be going well, even with my
husband and daughter tagging along because I was nursing. He
watched her while I interviewed with various faculty members,
met with the dean, and gave a job talk and a teaching demo. Despite the remarkable lack of sleep and baby in tow, I was hopeful
about my chances of getting the job. I realized that I knocked the
teaching demo out of the park when I heard a faculty member tell
the chair that students would rush to sign up for my classes. The
chair seemed to think I would get the job. I knew this because he
told me so. That's why I was so surprised when everything started
to take a turn.

At lunch with faculty members, the chair, and the dean, I made
harmless small talk, the kind of chitchat that academics love about

what they research and teach. At least, it all seemed harmless until a lull in the conversation when a woman lecturer asked: "If you take the job, what would your poor husband do?"

I was startled by her question, but I was more unnerved by the reaction of the faculty and the dean, all of whom turned to look at me as if to judge how I would respond. I looked back at them, and some of the faculty refused to meet my eyes. Lunch had come to a screeching halt. I took a deep breath and responded in a cheerful voice: "My poor husband will just have to figure it out."

Some folks chuckled at my directness, while others shifted uncomfortably in their seats. After lunch, the chair entered damage control mode and apologized profusely for such an inappropriate question. He informed me that the offending instructor did not represent the department and assured me that my marital status had *no impact* on my candidacy. I had a creeping suspicion that much of his concern was about how I reacted to the question about my marital status rather than it being asked. It was the kind of question that is supposed to be off-limits for all employers because it can lead to discriminatory hiring practices. He apologized some more, and I started to doubt my prospects about the job.

That my marriage was a line of inquiry for a job rather than my credentials rattled me. I assumed I would be judged on merit, on the strength of my qualifications, on the publications listed on my CV, not the fact that I was married. This was not the first or last time my assumptions about how academia worked would be proven wrong.

Weeks later, the chair called to tell me that I didn't get the job.

During the awkward phone call, the chair explained that I had impressed the department, but they just wanted to go in a "different direction." They hired a recently graduated (and recently married) white man in a subfield that wasn't even preferred in the job announcement. I ended the call as soon as I could. That visit was the last of three campus visits I had in 2008. I came in second twice; there was no tenure-track job for me.

But my experience with this particular department at this particular university suggested that getting a tenure-track job wouldn't be as easy as my adviser kept suggesting. I started to have doubts about my candidacy, not because of my qualifications but because of my identity. I was a white woman who happened to be a wife and mother. *What if who I was mattered more than what I accomplished?*

The disastrous lunch stuck with me. I couldn't help but wonder if the mere mention of my husband had pushed the search committee into a different *direction*. I couldn't help but think about the impact of taking a

nursing baby to my campus visits. Did the careless mention of my marriage plant doubts about whether I would take a position if offered? Did my
beautiful baby girl make me seem like a less serious candidate? *No*, I told
myself late at night while rocking and nursing my daughter, *that mention
was just an anomaly*. I tried to convince myself that I was just paranoid. I
would apply for jobs again next year. Clearly, this concern over my husband
would only happen this one time.

Soon, I realized that this gendered concern was not an anomaly at all.

During my five years on the academic job market, my marital status
kept popping up in preliminary interviews, campus visits, and even in discussions with my letter writers. I couldn't get away from discussions of my
husband or my kid.

"What would your poor husband do?" emerged as a refrain in my job
search. One of my recommenders repeatedly asked whether I would take
jobs if they were offered; he worried profusely about recommending me
for jobs that he thought I wouldn't take because of my husband and daughter. I spent much time assuring him that my career came first, even as I
knew that wasn't entirely true, so he would continue to write for me.

Later, I wondered if my colleagues who were married men had to en-
dure similar conversations. Did their spouses figure so heavily in the cal-
culations of recommenders and interviewers? Were their wedding rings
analyzed and mentioned in interviews? Were their poor wives influencing
possible job offers? Did their children factor into employers' discussions of
their credentials?

Apparently not. Writing in the *New York Times*, English professor Caroline Bicks describes how her husband emerged as a "problem" in her job
search, whereas no one ever asked him about his wife. "It felt as if my
wedding ring was a hurdle I had to clear to prove my commitment to academia," she writes, "while Brendon's was a badge of stability and good-guy
gravitas."[1]

What I, unfortunately, learned was that search committees seem far too
preoccupied with the marital status of women candidates and often seek
that information through indirect channels, as Female Science Professor
notes in the *Chronicle of Higher Education*. Like me, "zero" was the number
of times she was *not* asked about her husband.[2] How, then, should women

1. Caroline Bicks, "Is the Husband Going to Be a Problem?" *New York Times*,
August 12, 2010, http://www.nytimes.com/2010/08/15/fashion/15love.html?page
wanted=all&_r=0.

2. Female Science Professor, "The A to Z of Dual-Career Couples," *Chronicle*

manage this common, albeit "illegal" question? She advises answering and redirecting the conversation. Answering might plant doubts, but refusing to answer signals something more frightening for search committees: a two-body problem.

The two-body problem is, as Matt Reed nicely puts it, "an inelegant term" for "the difficulty that couples have in finding good jobs for both people that are geographically close enough that they can continue to live together."[3] Of course, the term and the issue aren't exactly new. Academic couples have long faced an uncomfortable choice: Let both partners maximize their careers, at the expense of living separately, or compromise one partner's position to stay together. What's different now is that there are so few tenure-track academic jobs—many of them in remote locations—for so many academic couples. What's more, women are more likely than men to have academic partners, according to a 2008 report, *Dual Career Academic Couples: What Universities Need to Know*, by Stanford University's Michelle R. Clayman Institute for Gender Research. Women usually bear the brunt of the two-body problem. I know I did.

Not only was I a wife and mother during my job search, but my husband, Chris, was also an academic, a computational scientist. It was never about navigating just my career as an academic; rather, we've had to navigate two careers and apply for academic jobs since we both graduated in 2008.

Marriage, however, affected our job searches differently: it was a liability for mine and a boon for his. Hiring committees imagined Chris as the head of household, someone who needed a job to support his wife and child. Academia's masculine bias was on full display. Men wanted to hire Chris because of his credentials but also because he was a man like them. They offered him more money in salary negotiations because of his family.

Hiring committees imagined me as a flight risk. (Though in one of Chris's earlier interviews, a hiring manager thought he was a flight risk because I was an academic too.) Interviewers viewed my academic strivings as hobbies, something I did but would eventually abandon for my marriage and family. Chris appeared as a serious candidate, but I, somehow, didn't. We both went on the job market determined to do what was best for our family, which meant staying together rather than living separately.

---

of Higher Education, July 4, 2011, http://www.chronicle.com/article/The-A-to-Z-of-Dual-Career/128096/.

3. Matt Reed, "Isolation and Jobs," *Inside Higher Ed*, September 20, 2013, https://www.insidehighered.com/blogs/confessions-community-college-dean/isolation-and-jobs#sthash.x28NsHFE.dpbs.

And before long, I, the humanities PhD, became the trailing spouse—first an adjunct and then a full-time lecturer. I thought if only I kept adding lines to my CV that I would finally get the tenure-track job I dreamed of. I thought that my book winning an award would help. I thought teaching interesting topics to packed classrooms would matter. I thought I could "hard work" my way into the tenure track, but I couldn't. Merit and accolades couldn't outweigh marriage and motherhood. Who search committees thought I was mattered more than what I accomplished.

After five years on the humanities job market and my second child on the way, I decided to take a break from academia. Chris decided to leave higher ed altogether and go work at a tech start-up. I started a new career as a freelance writer covering gender and higher education, and what I found shocked me.

My experiences coincided neatly with the data on married women and academic jobs. In *Do Babies Matter?* Mary Ann Mason and her coauthors show that in general women are 7 percent less likely to get a tenure-track job than are men. Married women fare even worse: they're 17 percent less likely than their unmarried peers to end up on the tenure track. (And the deck is even more stacked against married academic women with children, who are 21 percent less likely than a candidate without children to end up on the tenure track.)[4]

Marriage and children clearly affect women pursuing academic careers, especially since search committees seem to buy into outdated, gendered notions of work and family. Facing a harrowing job market, sexist assumptions about work-life balance, and cultural expectations about marriage and motherhood, women who are part of academic couples find ourselves in a bind. Do you seek two jobs and live apart? Do you stay with your partner and risk unemployment? Do you abandon academia altogether? What comes to matter more: the career that you trained years for or the life you are trying to build?

Plenty of folks felt the need to warn me about my choices after I made them. Colleagues advised me to not wear my wedding ring (or to wear my wedding ring), to pretend that my daughter didn't exist, to pretend that my husband didn't exist, and to attempt to remove any mention of my marriage from social media. (I pretty much refused to pretend my family didn't

4. Kelly J. Baker, "Are Children Career Killers?" *Chronicle Vitae*, June 8, 2014, https://chroniclevitae.com/news/569-are-children-career-killers; Mary Ann Mason, Nicholas H. Wolfinger, and Marc Goulden, *Do Babies Matter? Gender and Family in the Ivory Tower* (New Brunswick, NJ: Rutgers University Press, 2013).

exist.) A tenure-track professor at the state university where I worked as a lecturer explained that "I did it wrong" by getting married and having a kid before I went on the job market. "Everyone," she continued, "knew that you had to wait to get married and have kids until you got that tenure-track offer." That's what she did, so her choice appeared as the only real option. My department chair sat me down in her office to clarify my options for my academic career: some day soon, I would have to choose between my career and my family. She made it seem as if it would be impossible to have both.

The already complicated two-body problem seemed even more thorny to navigate when academics offered such gendered career advice. It seemed that my choices were limited because everyone already took them out of my hands.

I couldn't get a tenure-track job because search committees couldn't look beyond my wedding ring. My CV couldn't make up for the assumptions that they made about me, not as a scholar, but as a wife and mother. I never had a tenure-track offer.

I followed my husband because I never had a chance to stay in academia, and I might have stayed. This is typical of the two-body problem, as Mason warns: "One body must defer to the other's career and that body is far more likely to be the woman's."[5] I was that body, and so were many women scholars that I knew.

The Clayman Institute report found that women were far more likely than men to consider their partner's employment prospects, often at the expense of their own. In fact, many women sacrificed professional mobility or refused jobs on account of their partner's employment offers (or lack thereof), while at all ranks, men prioritized their own careers over those of their partners.

Not surprisingly, then, the survey found that most of the men surveyed got the plum appointments, while their wives got short shrift. When couples were recruited together, 58 percent of the "first hires" (the ones more likely to get the tenure-track positions) were men, while 74 percent of the "second hires" were women. For those women, the consolation prize often was a non-tenure-track position and the stigma of the "trailing spouse," which is the assumption that the second hire is not a "quality" candidate. Sadly, these figures correspond to the high proportion of women in contin-

5. Mary Ann Mason, "In the Ivory Tower, Men Only," *Slate*, June 17, 2013, http://www.slate.com/articles/double_x/doublex/2013/06/female_academics_pay_a_heavy_baby_penalty.html.

gent positions—and the lower proportion of women in tenure-track positions at research universities, too.

Academia still favors a single-earner household with high mobility. Since 86 percent of academics with stay-at-home partners were men, it's no surprise that men are assumed to be more mobile. Outdated notions of gender and career creep into interviews and hiring decisions. What this means is that unemployed and underemployed women leave academia, like I did. We find other careers, often alternative-academic (alt-ac) careers that keep us close to higher ed.

After a couple years of a break from academia, I decided to leave. Ironically, Chris was willing to quit his post and follow me to the ends of the Earth—or as far as Oklahoma, at least—if I got a tenure-track offer. No one ever asked what Chris was willing to give up for my career, but assumed that I would give up my career for him. My marriage and family outweighed my credentials again and again. We "solved" our two-body problem, just as many others like us have, by leaving academia.

The life we were building together mattered more than the careers that we thought we wanted to have.

Interview with Chris and Kelly Baker

Chris and I got married in between semesters during the senior year of our undergraduate studies. We had originally planned to wait for graduation, but—much to our parents' chagrin—we pushed up the date out of consideration for graduate school.

This harebrained idea was mine. I wanted us to enter our respective programs (religious studies for me, computational science for him) at the same university as a married couple, a unified front against whatever we might face. We negotiated two bodies and two careers from the beginning. We were concerned about how graduate school would affect our married life; what we didn't realize was the impact our marriage would have on our career options.

During graduate school, Chris was offered an internship in New Mexico, twenty-three hours away from our home in Florida. He accepted it, and we had a long-distance relationship for eleven of those twenty months. We became good at living separately. We missed each other, but the internship bettered Chris's CV and his job prospects (and the benefits of a real salary).

The distance was too much, so I left Florida to live with Chris. He continued his internship while finishing his dissertation. I taught as an adjunct while writing mine. The experience highlighted a fact that we had previously suspected: we weren't going to be content in a long-distance relationship. Moving back together was a temporary reprieve. The two-body problem soon caught up with us again when we both entered the job market. The two of us will split the story from here.

Kelly: So we decided to enter the job market at the same time to see what kinds of jobs were available, but we also prioritized staying together. What happened is that we had interviews in very different locations, ranging from the East Coast to the Pacific Northwest. In each place, we tried to figure out if there might be jobs for each of us.

Chris: It was a great time! Every time you sent off a job packet, I would spend a few days on Zillow looking at real estate. After all, my dissertation was done and Angry Birds hadn't been invented yet.

Kelly: It was not a great time! From our first moments on the job market, I was hopeful that I might find a tenure-track job, but I was also afraid that my career might always come second because your degree was favored by academia and industry. Moreover, I feared we might have to live separately to pursue our careers. Otherwise, one of us might have to defer, and it seemed that it would be me. I also didn't want to be a woman who gave up her career for her husband's. What I eventually realized is that decisions about careers are never as easy as they might appear. There are so many factors to consider, including relationships and family. The life we hoped to build included much more than our careers.

When did you first realize that two academics might have a problem finding jobs in proximity to one another?

Chris: For the first few years, our two-body problem was *apparently* a hypothetical one. My understanding of the two-body problem at the time was similar to Wikipedia's current definition: that situation where two sufficiently significant others are presented with career opportunities that are incoincident. (The Wikipedia authors were thoughtful enough to present a list of solutions; if only we'd read that page sooner. . . .) We never had simultaneous job offers.

Kelly: It would have been much easier for you to find a job with a PhD in computational science, so you were supportive of my job hunt and willing to leave your postdoc to follow me. Looking back at my early years on the market, I'm sort of in awe of your tireless support. You were always in my corner encouraging me to apply for any job that I wanted to. I think you were even willing to move to Oklahoma for me. (Seriously, Oklahoma?) You seemed ready to move and start another career if I found a tenure-track position. Why?

Chris: Part of it was the logical realization that jobs in religious studies were going to be relatively hard to come by. Which isn't to say that there were a ton of jobs "in" computational science; alas, the curse of interdisciplinary training befell me. Still, by virtue of my academic training and work experience, it did seem that there would be a greater number of opportunities for employment, whether in industry, government, or academia. When it became apparent that some of the tenure-track jobs you were applying for were receiving literally hundreds of applications, it seemed foolish to turn anything down. Solve the hard problem first, right? In the worst-case scenario (Oklahoma?), I could always go back to grad school. If at first you don't succeed. . . .

Kelly: Two PhDs are plenty for our household. Really.

While you were willing to follow me, search committees seemed to assume the opposite: that I would defer my career for yours. On every campus visit I ever had, I was asked about my husband and what he would do if we moved. Assumptions about traditional gender norms appear to be alive and well in academia. As a married woman, my candidacy seemed predicated on how my husband might react to a job offer. I was completely gobsmacked by this attitude. I assumed that academics, of all people, would not perpetuate gender stereotypes, but I was wrong. So. Wrong.

How did others react to your desire to follow me? How did hiring committees treat you when they realized your wife was also an academic?

Chris: For the most part, there wasn't a lot of concern. I primarily applied for jobs in industry and at government labs. My marital (and, ultimately, paternal) circumstances were occasionally discussed (per HR policies, under my own disclosure). When this happened, managers and interviewers both seemed quite content with the explanation that my spouse would be able to find a job nearby.

All my interviews were in multi-university cities. However, there is something to be said about convincing yourself that the candidate that you want to hire is going to accept the job. In my experience (both from the inside and the outside), academic hiring committees seem to treat the hiring process much more personally than do industry managers—this is "our" tenure-track position that we're handing out, after all. Industry and lab jobs exist because there is work that needs to be done and they need someone to do it; most academic search committees don't seem to share that urgency.

There were some outliers for me, however. In particular, a manager at one of the national labs where I interviewed repeatedly expressed concern over the possibility that my spouse would force us to move after he'd gone through the personal trouble of hiring me. He was a former academic.

Kelly: My marital status, unfortunately, became a key part of my candidacy. Perhaps I should have never worn my wedding ring. Yet I wanted to be honest about who I was. Additionally, no one ever advised me that my marriage might become a problem to potential employers before I graduated with a PhD. No one gave me the "hide your husband and kids" talk, which I still find to be a problematic method to manage sexism. Being expected to pretend that you don't have a partner or family is unreasonable. In hindsight, it might have been a terrible idea to wear my ring and signal my marriage. Do you remember how much we talked about whether I should wear my ring? Did you even consider hiding your marital status?

Chris: I recall this wedding ring discussion coming up in the later years, after you'd had a couple of telling conversations around the subject. But in the early years, I don't think it was something that I was aware of as a potential problem. In the interviews I had where I didn't know anyone, the discussions about family were positive.

Kelly: So marriage and fatherhood made you appear more stable, while marriage and motherhood seemed to erode my competence and accomplishments. Maybe search committees feared I would refuse their job offer or that I would request a hire for my husband. I can't really know why I didn't get offers, but the focus on my husband couldn't have helped. The irony, of course, is that I would have taken any of the jobs I applied for, even if it was in Oklahoma, and we had already decided that I wouldn't negotiate a dual hire. No one ever asked me what I was willing to do, but they did ask repeatedly about my husband. In one conference interview, search committee members even implied that my research was more like a hobby than a job.

Talking about these incidents still makes me so angry. My CV, hard work, and assurances of mobility couldn't balance out the threat of my wedding ring. What I now know is that there are plenty of studies that expose the bias against married women in academia; I just didn't realize this during my many years on the job market. Our two-body problem never became a problem. It was pretty much resolved because I never received a job offer.

Chris: The two-body problem as we currently understand it is actually a three-body problem, involving the applicant, the significant other, and the hiring committee, and describing a peculiar system in which one of the bodies is often repulsive to another. Unfortunately, as Wikipedia tells it, though three-body problems have been studied for hundreds of years, they do not in general permit an analytical solution.

Kelly: Imagining this as a three-body problem is a more accurate reflection of the actual problem. While the two-body problem lays the blame on the couple, this is really a problem, as you note, for the couple and the employing institutions. The two-body problem appears as a result of the couple's choices, which it partially is, but it's also compounded by the attitudes of hiring committees and their institutions. More importantly, this is also a gendered issue, and there needs to be more reflection about the consequences to candidates and institutions.

So, we did most of those interviews a couple of years ago. Since then, you've changed jobs a few times (there's an unfair amount of love for computer science PhDs), and I've shifted from part-time freelance writer to full-time to now editor of *Women in Higher Education*. I've been thinking about how we solved the two-body problem by removing our bodies from academia. What do you think about that?

Chris: The problem is not unique to academia. It's certainly made more difficult by the fact that most university towns only have a single university, and most academics can hope to find a tenure-track job in only very few departments. Contrast this against other careers with special training, like attorneys or GP physicians or schoolteachers, where most reasonable cities will host a larger number of different potential employers.

When two folks restrict themselves to applying for tenure-track jobs at universities, which the standard narrative tells us is necessary to be considered successful, then they've accepted this problem. Unfortunately, as we've seen in the past few years, this isn't the only place where the standard narrative lets us down. It's increasingly difficult for qualified candidates to find tenure-track jobs, to the extent that everyone is having to look outside the university. I wonder whether this situation, plus the additional pressure on partnered academics, is going to result in more folks thinking outside the quad to solve this problem.

Kelly: Thinking outside the quad is a great way to think about it. So many of us are looking beyond colleges and universities for work because we're trying to find a career, or maybe just a job, that allows us to live the lives we want to, not the lives that are expected of us. I realized early on that our family's quality of life mattered deeply to me, to both of us, and that academia didn't care about my life or my family or my mental and physical health. I had to find a career outside academia, which at first seemed super daunting. But, there are so many options beyond academia for PhDs, if only we start to consider what our academic work trains us for beyond the tenure track. When I first started applying for jobs outside academia, I began to realize that teaching, research, and writing could all be broken down into smaller skills that employers were interested in. I had abilities that made me appealing to employers, but first I had to recognize what they were.

Now years later, what advice would you give to dual-career couples?

Chris: The career advice that I would give recent PhDs is the same advice that I would give anyone in a long-term relationship: if you want to be happy, you're going to need to be flexible. I suppose my prescription for dual-career couples is a double dose of flexibility. Fixing your happiness to strict ideals is not a good recipe for success. And academia, like many other industries, isn't specifically concerned about your happiness.

Kelly: Academia doesn't give a shit about your happiness or your life, which was sort of liberating to recognize. What I want folks considering alt-ac careers to know is: *Lives matter more than careers.* Focus on building the life you want rather than pursuing the career that people think you should have. Our lives matter more than our commitment to academia. They always have, but sometimes, it can take a while to realize it.

7

Reframing Success

RACHEL LEVENTHAL-WEINER

When I started graduate school over a decade ago, I felt like a fish out of water. Newly married, in my very late twenties, self-conscious about whether I could hack the program, I felt constantly behind the younger, fresher members of my cohort. I knew that I needed to feel secure in my choice to pursue this degree later than others around me. To me, security is having a plan. I conjured a loose vision of my future work life: studying schools and inequality, I hoped to end up teaching in a department of sociology or a school of education and engaged with local schools. I felt doubtful I would pursue a tenure-track path and was skeptical of the ivory tower version of sociology. When you study schools and kids, you want consciousness raising and change. I wanted to do real work, and while academic scholarship is real, its reach felt limited.

That was the extent of my concrete aspirations.

Graduate school, mentors, advisers, and classmates taught me quickly that planning is useful but sometimes futile. Your life takes unexpected turns, and events interrupt productivity and progress. And your plan may shift, morph, and ultimately not stand up to the life you have when you're finished with graduate school. I learned that your professional life is always happening and the process of finding your next opportunity is iterative and not linear. And finally, I learned to expect imperfection out of every job I have.

Delay That Decision until after You Have Tenure or Not

Whether I acknowledge it or not, I forged my path out of the academy as I was accepting my offer of admission to the sociology PhD program at the University of Connecticut. In my first conversation with the director of the graduate program, I immediately asked about maternity leave for graduate students rather than coursework or comprehensive exams. Deciding when and how to expand our family was the first (and perhaps heaviest) decision I faced as a graduate student.

Her response: "Many people decide to wait until after they have a job or earn tenure. Some people choose to have children earlier."

What if that job never came? The state of the job market was already precarious at the start of graduate school, and the onset of the Great Recession certainly didn't help matters. As someone who studies schooling at all levels, I did not trust tenure. I knew then that I was not willing to risk it.

I was in a decidedly different stage of life than other people in my cohort. I was twenty-eight years old and had already worked in two industries and earned a master's degree. My husband and I married the summer before I started my PhD program, and rather than continue to rent our apartment, we were looking for a home to buy. Some time in the next six years, we hoped there would be a baby.

So classes started. I worried a lot about being taken seriously in my first year. I don't know if that was because I was older than most others or because I didn't study sociology as an undergraduate. I felt impatient and overwhelmed at the same time—impatient that I wanted to get to the work I wanted to do and overwhelmed because I wanted others to see me as a serious scholar. My friends who weren't in graduate school were hitting their stride in their own careers, and here I was taking a huge step back. I kept reminding myself that studying the sociology of education and working toward equity in education for all students was my path in life. It was what got me out of bed in the morning and flooded my thoughts all day. And there was (and still is) no shortage of good work to be done.

Months passed, and I settled into a routine. I felt more at ease in class discussions and worried less about perfection in my work and in my performance. I started to wrap my head around the next five to six years. Just as things started to fall into place, everything changed in an instant.

It was toward the end of spring semester, and after months of anxiety over my Contemporary Theory course, I was finally feeling comfortable about speaking up in class. Over dinner one night I was describing a particular day's discussion to my husband. The phone rang. It was a fated call from my father to let me know that my mother had been struck by a car and that she was in intensive care. He didn't tell me on the phone call that the prognosis was not good. We packed up and hauled out of our apartment. Several hours later when we arrived at the hospital, we learned that she was not showing signs of brain activity and was not likely to come out of her coma. It was my worst nightmare.

This was real life. It was as real as life was ever going to be. I immediately seceded from all life obligations, and everyone was understanding. Given the circumstances of my mother's death, no one blinked an eye. Everyone, including my adviser, the director of my graduate program, colleagues, and friends told me to focus on my family and return to life when I was ready. As it was, my mother's death had come as a complete surprise just six weeks before my sister's wedding. It was a very stressful time, and I needed to be present for my family.

My mother's death showed me that we have no control over the short or long term. Losing her sharpened my perspective on the near future and the choice to expand our family. I admitted to myself that my personal life had to be as important as my professional life, and I did not want to prioritize the possibility of a professional arrangement that might never happen. The things you choose to establish a life—a home, friendships, family, self-care—I wanted those things.

I knew for sure that I did not want to live a life that felt like I was on hold forever.

A Sociologist or an Education Researcher

Though I put my life on hold that summer, eventually I found a way to tie up the loose ends of my first year. As my second year started, the end of the road felt a long way off. I could barely envision what the end of the road looked like, but it was clear from the first day of my program: a sociologist's holy grail job is a tenure-track position (with bonus points for a prestigious institution). And whether I realized it at the time, despite the setbacks I experienced in my first year, I projected myself as an ambitious Research 1 (R1) tenure-track kind of person even though I was not sure that was my ultimate aspiration. I did not know how to communicate what I needed, and I noticed immediately that achieving anything other than an R1 tenure-track position was considered a consolation prize. Worse yet, based on the reactions from faculty members, expressing interest in anything other than the holy grail seemed to be ill-advised.

I kept waiting to feel that I wanted to be a full-time forever scholar. I ticked off milestones, defending my thesis prospectus and working through my comp exams. And even though I might have given off a tenure-track vibe, every time I appeared before a committee of inquisitors, I wanted to shrivel up and hide. I could not stand the exercise of proving my value in front of a firing squad of future colleagues.

I was engaged with research projects as a research assistant, but it wasn't until I took a research workshop that I engaged with the full publishing process. I spent a fair amount of time with one of my mentors in the process—he typically mentored men, and in one of our conversations, he interrupted some diatribe of mine to pose the question: sociologist or education researcher? I didn't see a distinction and would have been happy with either outcome, but his forced choice exercise prompted a newfound alertness about the status hierarchy.

And then he posed another question, "What will your husband do when you're on the job market?" The idea that we would prioritize a job for me when I earned a fraction of my husband's salary seemed preposterous. I didn't have a good answer, so I brushed it off. But the questions lingered for weeks, even months, as I tried to decide between sociologist or education researcher and as I wondered how we would handle both our careers. I did not have any answers.

Due Date: March (the Imperfect Academic Baby)

Before the start of my third year, I got pregnant. The pregnancy was wanted, though we did not anticipate the timing. I was simultaneously overjoyed and terrified: overjoyed at the prospect of becoming a parent and terrified at the idea of telling my adviser and my committee that I was expecting a baby. My immediate expectation was to defend myself as dedicated, committed, and serious. My adviser, it turned out, was happy and enthusiastic and also expecting a baby herself.

My pregnancy proceeded without incident, and I was subject to the kind of quiet humiliation one experiences as a pregnant student. Negotiating our sprawling campus was exhausting. Off campus, if strangers saw me lumbering, rushing, or struggling, they would give up their seat, hold the door for me, or simply smile. On a campus full of self-absorbed students, I stood on bus rides to the outskirts of the commuter parking lot and then schlepped over to my car. I could not fit in desks and dreaded the three flights of stairs in the ADA-unfriendly building where I kept my office. In the mailroom, a young male faculty member gestured toward my growing belly and asked "What's going on here?" as though he'd never seen a pregnant woman before or was too nervous to ask me if I was expecting. Mentors mentioned "my condition" or "my state" as though I was a "girl in trouble" in 1957, instead of a grown, married woman. Others simply stared.

If I had thought my mother's death was a tectonic shift in my life, nothing prepared me for the birth of my daughter. I was induced on my daughter's due date, two days after proctoring a final. I graded papers while I was
in labor. I was midway through a complex methods class I was taking in
another department. I had thought through many of my choices about the
semester, but there were still many unanswered questions.

Our daughter was born after twenty-eight hours of labor, including
one botched epidural resulting in a spinal migraine. The first ten days of
recovery from labor and delivery while trying to nurse were excruciating.
I could barely lift my head because of the spinal migraine, which causes
searing pain from changes in pressure and elevation (it would take ten
minutes to sit halfway up in bed), and my entire body throbbed in pain
from trying to nurse. My baby was calm and loving. She was snuggly and
slept well.

I struggled during those initial weeks. I felt like I was in a cloud, and yet
a small part of me felt tethered to this journey I was on. I had colleagues
and friends with true maternity leave who could fully detach from their
work. Though I was able to take a longer maternity leave (without pay),
I felt like the demands of my graduate program constantly nagged me,
tickling my brain when I tried to be at ease with my baby. And unlike the
space I was allowed with my mother's death, when the baby was born I felt
(consciously or unconsciously) that I was failing my committee, my cohort,
my program by making this choice to prioritize my family. The graduate
program is not built to accommodate calamity. Nor is it built to accommodate women, quite frankly. The program hinges on a level of detachment
from the corporeal, on a laser focus and dedication to one's intellectual
development.

Losing my mother made me question, doubt, and ultimately discover a
source of inner strength, and becoming a mother emboldened that for me.
And while I felt turned upside down, struggling to get a grip on my new
responsibilities, working to fit together the puzzle pieces in our lives (who
picks up; who drops off; who gives the bath, makes the meals, dresses the
boo boos), I didn't doubt whether I could do it. Grief had taught me that
strength was there.

Academic versus Nonprofit Work

As I settled back into graduate life, my department started ratch-
eting up their professional development. All students complete a prosem-
inar series in their first year, but students began asking (nay, pleading) for

more support during the academic year to prepare for the job market. All discussion focused solely on the academic job market, with a penchant for a research university position. The focus was so narrow that careers in community colleges were not even considered. I began to see and understand the writing on the wall—getting interviews was based solely on your CV, and your CV would only be populated with publications if your star had been hitched to a productive senior scholar (or you were productive yourself). There was a correlation between top-tier programs and productivity, and I was in no position to be competitive on the job market. Your value was based on your scholarly production. The idea that scholarship would be the only metric used to judge my value, no matter how much I excelled as an educator and adviser, was a tough pill to swallow.

The summer after my daughter turned one, I had the opportunity to take on a fellowship outside the academy in a nonprofit advocacy group. I had contacted them after hearing their executive director speak on the local public radio station. I was able to leverage my experience and skills into a summer position that paid me better than my graduate stipend during the school year. When I reached out to my adviser to solicit her thoughts, she expressed some hesitation but reluctantly approved, saying, "Just don't let it interfere with your work." In this brief but meaningful interaction, I learned that the only real work is scholarly work, and this other work represented a distraction.

Distraction or not, it was a game-changer. The summer gave me exposure to nonprofit work, to a new kind of professional arrangement, and to the opportunity to start networking to understand how a PhD could help me outside the academy. And it was not one specific interaction but the sum total of the experience that got the wheels turning in my head.

When the summer ended, I used the momentum to start building a social network, conducting informational interviews, and gathering information about nonacademic employment. In one interview, I learned that intellectual property may be an issue in some nonprofit research organizations. In another interview, I discovered the benefits that more traditional office-oriented work culture can yield for a parent of young children. Every conversation gave me a new perspective on what my work life could be like, and I began to think about my "dream" job.

I never discussed this social networking and informational interviewing with my own adviser, and I regret never having an open and honest conversation with my adviser or my committee about my post–grad school plans. It was simply assumed that what I wanted to do was pursue a tenure-track (most likely Research 1) position. My adviser was in the process of earning tenure herself and was burdened with the extra stress of proving her value while also shepherding me through my own training. And even though I was her only student, we never did speak frankly about my aspirations. It was ironic, because my subject of study included students' postsecondary aspirations, and yet we never discussed my own.

Mediocre at Everything

I learned both from implicit and explicit messages that in order to be considered a serious scholar, you do not speak of your family. Whether I realized it or not, I always led with my family. I was quick to throw in a cute story about the baby or lament something with my husband. I remain happily married and the radiant mother of two little girls, and I am proud of those facts. I thought that staying silent about them was awkward and disingenuous, but at a national conference, I tried to act the part of an academic and discovered that I wasn't fooling anyone.

At that national conference, a renowned sociologist proffered the worst life advice I have ever heard: be prepared for mediocrity. This woman decried her own parenting, the imposition her family placed on her scholarly productivity, and the burden marriage presented to her life. Although she might well be right about the challenges of work-life balance in the academy, painting it so negatively rubbed me the wrong way. The academy is not designed to accommodate women, families, or the demands of modern life. Trying to balance parenthood and scholarship are difficult enough for men, but women struggle exponentially harder to prove their value, their legitimacy, and their dedication. Settling for mediocrity in everything but academic work is an insufficient solution to juggling work and family life.

During my fifth year, I became pregnant with my second baby. The news of this second pregnancy was tolerated by my committee, but I would not describe their reaction as overjoyed. Many members of our department were parents of one child and could not understand my decision to expand our family. I was struggling to finish my dissertation prospectus, and I failed to carry it over the finish line before my youngest daughter was born.

Because we welcomed her in July, I received no financial support or paid leave from our university. Graduate student maternity leave is only guaranteed when classes are in session. Without a child care plan that would allow me to teach that fall, I took a semester of unpaid leave.

Unlike after my first pregnancy, nothing was tugging me back to school. Our finances took a hit, but I was happy to be home with the baby and fully detached from my work. I knew I would have to finish eventually, but for the first time I wondered whether I would be able to finish at all. One thing I did know: when I returned, I would be teaching my own sections, writing (and hopefully defending) my dissertation prospectus, and edging closer to the finish line. At a time when I would need to be more focused than ever on my work, I also knew that pretending that my family was not important or not worthy of my time and focus was not possible for me.

Geographically Constrained

Staring down a complicated set of responsibilities during my seventh (and final) year of graduate school, I sent my CV to every institution of higher education within fifty miles. A strange chain of events landed my CV in the Educational Studies Program at Trinity College, where their chair encouraged me to apply for a visiting professor position. I did. I interviewed by phone. I heard nothing for weeks. And then a call, an interview, and a job offer all within twenty-four hours.

I spent three years at Trinity College. During my first year, I finished my PhD program and earned my degree. That first year was a marathon, prepping two new courses and learning a new institution while writing furiously. I set a firm deadline at the end of April and backed out of intervening deadlines. My progress depended on my ability to write, and my ability to write depended on the cooperation of my two small girls, my husband, and my new students. My ability to pay attention to everyone slowly waned over the year until the final weeks before I completed my draft for defense. I saw myself abdicate the focus I usually maintained on my family and prioritize the writing, and I hated how it made me feel. Weekends were spent watching my husband manage the girls, so I could put the final pieces together. But with a few days to spare, my committee agreed to a defense, and the defense and edits proceeded without incident. And on Mother's Day in 2013, I earned the coveted title of Dr.

In my second year, I spent time networking and learning. And in my final year, I began to plan my next move. At Trinity I developed a practice of saying "yes." My appointment in the Educational Studies Program was all about community engagement, teaching students about schools and schooling while working with local organizations and schools. It was as close as I would ever be to my long-term goal set way back at the beginning of graduate school. I sat on committees, attended professional development and intellectual development opportunities, networked inside and outside the college, and tried to leverage every dollar they were willing to spend on faculty. The unique part of my experience was that while there were many things open just to full-time, long-term faculty, contingent faculty members could sometimes reap similar benefits. There was a meager budget to support travel to one conference and the chance to earn stipends through service with students or on committees. So I said "yes" to as much as I could.

Though I was doing the work I dreamed about, there was no future in it. My chair made that clear when I interviewed, saying, "This is a temporary position—anything is possible, but what I know now is that there is no promise of a permanent position." I started to feel embedded and yet, as I rounded into my third and final year, I knew I would have to start planning my next move. I was starting to learn that the job search is never quite over.

One of my courses, Race, Class, and Education Policy, connected me to the state legislature, located in the same town as the college. I started to fall in love with policy advocacy and used the same informational interviewing strategy to amass connections, information, and ideas about organizations I could serve.

Not Knowing What It Will Be

When I started my position at Trinity, I was deciding whether to start blogging for myself. I was worried, frankly, that being too public about my thoughts on the academy, on tenure, and on parenthood would come back to bite me at some point. An outspoken friend, who is a published author, offered some of the best advice I have ever received: You don't know what it's going to be yet, so why hedge? Why try to control it? In September 2012, I began writing my own blog, Rogue Cheerios. I started writing about the possibility of leaving the academy, though I didn't know yet it would lead to writing about faculty and family life for *Vitae*. And in the process I rediscovered the joy in writing I had lost while producing my dissertation chapters.

I approached my professional life with the same attitude. Not knowing where I would land yet, I had no option but to plant loads and loads of seeds with no clear understanding of what, if anything, would bloom. Trinity led me to new local colleagues. Those colleagues connected me to other partners, and before long, I was hearing about possible job opportunities before I would see or hear of their posting. When a position as an education policy advocate opened up in a well-respected statewide think tank, I jumped at the opportunity.

A Good Fit

By the time I left Trinity and took the job at Connecticut Voices for Children, I was no longer conflicted about leaving the academy. I did not struggle with my identity as a professional, nor did I lament whether this would end my academic career forever. On the contrary, every step along the way solidified personal values and professional attributes that helped me make the decision to take a job. After my children were born, fitting them into the academic life seemed nearly impossible. And having weathered the traumatic loss of my own mother, I knew that academia left little wiggle room for personal calamity.

The contingent faculty position pushed me to question what kind of job I wanted. In the limited discussions I had with my adviser about my own aspirations, she affirmed that nonacademic work would be "a good fit for me." She said it in a way that implied I didn't fit in as a scholar. Or that's how I heard it. But leaning into this new position, I finally recognized my professional strengths in presenting, speaking, writing, and consulting. In taking this new job, I finally felt like I could exhale and be genuine about who I was as a professional rather than resist and force myself into the mold of a capital-A Academic.

Juggling the demands of my final semester of teaching while easing into a new job at the think tank, I was thrilled at the prospect of getting close to policy making. The work was perfect for me, but I encountered too many challenges to make the position a long-term possibility. Between a challenging leader and several conflicts in expectations, I did not have the tools or the support I needed to do the job well. I had a long commute, and during the first six months I finished off my contract with Trinity while working "part-time" at the advocacy organization. I was learning a lesson that any professional—academic or not—encounters: sometimes the work is great, but the organization is not the best fit. And this would have been true of an academic job—you can find a dream department situated inside an institutional nightmare. And while my initial inclination was to depart quickly, I knew the position afforded me the chance to continue to expand my network, and I wanted to make a move for the right position.

Reframing Success

When I realized that I needed to find my next nonacademic job, at first I felt a little defeated. My move outside the academy taught me almost immediately that no job is perfect. I decided that my next move would have to be more calculated. If I was going to leave, I wanted to leave for the opportunity that seemed as close to "right" as possible.

The work I had done to establish my network, to meet partners and learn from colleagues began to pay off when I saw a job posting for a small nonprofit organization seeking someone with experience as an educator and researcher. The position seemed to call to me, but the qualifications were a little confusing. Rather than stay perplexed, I reached out to the executive director, someone I knew from my advocacy work, and set up time to talk. Our talk led to an interview, and the interview led to my current job.

And while my job is a great fit, it is not totally perfect. I sensed some red flags before I took the position and asked pointed questions about them. In the end, the position boasted better compensation and a shorter commute. My quality of life changed immeasurably. I didn't realize it, but I had been in a fog for months, unable to pull myself out. People asked me if I would miss teaching, but I am still teaching. People asked me if I would miss research, but now I get to serve as a consultant to incredible nonprofit and community organizations troubling their way through issues in their towns. I am teaching and working with local organizations, so in some ways I am close to achieving my original goals set at the start of graduate school.

Forging Ahead

My dissertation defense is four years in the rearview mirror. When I defended, I already had one foot out of the academy door, and I haven't looked back since. Though my initial plan left the door open for an academic path, I found and followed signals along the way that led me to my current work as an advocate and educator. I should have noted the very first of those signals—my own insistence on understanding maternity leave for graduate students—as a sign that a balance between work and family remained central to my life plan. I probably ignored those signals because I treated graduate school as a period of respite from professional life, when I should have seen it as part of the professional experience. These signals came over the course of my seven years in graduate school, and each tipped the proverbial scales in terms of the vision and values I held for future work.

First, I reject the constant forced choice exercise presented during graduate training: pick this specialty and you're forever aligned with a certain camp, choose teaching over research and you'll be regarded as less intellectual and more vocational, choose family over career and you'll never hack it as a true scholar, and worst of all, choose outside the academy and you'll close the door forever on your future scholarship. Your career is a long road, and nothing in life is guaranteed. Some choices require greater effort to overcome or undo, but few choices will dictate the entire arc of your career.

Second, prepare to constantly reorganize your priorities in life. The things that matter in life during your first year of graduate training may not be the same when you walk across the stage. This was certainly the case for me in ways I predicted and never anticipated. From my first year to the present day, I am constantly shuffling my priorities. All along, I have resisted the urge to feel disappointed when work or family or some other priority takes the top spot. Work and life is more shuffle or juggle than balance, like the game Whac-A-Mole. I tackle one thing and another rears up in its place, and it's never-ending.

Third, accept the flaws in all your professional experiences and learn from them rather than flee from them. I never thought I would find myself in a job where I doubted the leadership of the organization, but I did. No arrangement will be perfect, and how you work will depend largely on what you can tolerate. As in reorganizing your priorities, be honest about the flaws you can manage and the issues that will make work intolerable. And rather than run, find ways to learn and grow from those challenges.

Finally, and perhaps most importantly, this professional life is a long game. Don't worry about where you are in your own long game. No job—not even a tenure-track job—is secure. You have to remain hungry. Your professional life is always happening. Leaving is the first, tough step on a long, professional path. That transition out—to find distance between the work you thought you would do and the work you end up doing—can be the toughest. But the transition to the next job means that there is actually life after the academy.

There is no magic formula for leaving, and it is important to remember that you have agency. At the beginning of graduate school, I thought I could keep my professional and personal lives separate. Within a year of starting graduate school, my new husband and I would become homeowners. In that same year I would lose my mother unexpectedly. Twice in the course of my graduate program, we welcomed a new baby into our home. Life was happening whether I liked it or not, and though leaving the academy was not what I planned, my graduate training and exit from the academy were an exercise in embracing and accepting imperfection.

Leaving the academy is actually not the end of the story.

It is simply the beginning. . . .

RACHEL LEVENTHAL-WEINER

PART II

Creating New Careers

8

Manifesto: The Freelance Academic

KATIE ROSE GUEST PRYAL

In the new, corporate model of higher education, academics of all stripes, but most commonly those in contingent positions, find themselves pushed to the margins—of their departments, of their very institutions. If you're lucky enough to have a contingent full-time position, you often still feel like an outsider. If you are an adjunct, then you almost certainly do. And even if you have a tenured or tenure-track position, if you aren't a lifeboater with your head in an unmentionable place, then you can probably see that the system you are part of is unsustainable.[1] Its future is rocky. You might worry that you'll need to relocate some day—and what will you do then, when there aren't any tenured jobs to be found?

Welcome to the new world of the Freelance Academic. I write about that world in my columns of the same name for *Chronicle Vitae*.[2] This chapter tells the story of my transition from a patchwork, contingent career in academia to one in which I decided to approach my academic career as a freelancer—with all the benefits

Earlier versions of the writing in this chapter previously appeared in *Chronicle Vitae*: "A Manifesto for the Freelance Academic" (*Vitae*, October 31, 2014), "The University Is Just Another Client" (*Vitae*, February 5, 2015), and "Can Adjuncts Be Freelancers?" (*Vitae*, July 24, 2015).

1. Higher education blogger Jason Tebbe coined the term "lifeboater" back in 2013: "These are junior scholars who don't bother thinking about the naked exploitation of a system where adjuncts are paid as little as $1,700 a course, and do just as good of a job (or better) as they do. In their minds, they won, they're on the lifeboat, and fuck all those other people drowning around them."

2. You can read all the columns of the series online at *Chronicle Vitae*, http://bit.ly/freelance-academic.

that come with that approach. After all, the universities I worked for already treated me like one.

The decision was incredibly freeing. And now that I've moved away from academia altogether, working completely for myself, I build on the freelance career moves I made when I was still in the academy. This chapter will teach you how to start making those moves, too.

But first: what drove me to look for something more than the work that I was doing day-to-day in academia? I came to a realization, one that many others have had as well. The realization went something like this.

As scholars and teachers, we work in overstressed conditions with inadequate resources, many of us hoping that somehow—someday—the academic world will right itself again. But the academic world isn't going to right itself again. It's changing, and it's not going to change back.

There aren't enough jobs for the large number of graduate students finishing up their degrees. The jobs are depleted for a couple of reasons, but the main one is this: even though college enrollment is higher than it used to be, colleges are relying more and more on contingent labor rather than full-time, tenured labor with benefits and job security. To survive in this changing academic world in which institutions treat (most) academics as disposable, I realized that we, as academics, have to change too.

So one day, when I'd had enough, I wrote my opening salvo—a five-point Freelance Academic Manifesto—and published it on my blog. Later, *Vitae* republished it as a column. That was back in 2014.

The purpose of the manifesto was to help contingent professors (and all professors who are feeling woefully disempowered by their higher education employment) take some power back. As a contingent professor, I first put together this list to help myself make work decisions in the new academic paradigm. I felt like I'd lost my navigational points, so I created new ones. As I wrote these navigational points, I relied heavily on a new community I built, using the alternative-academic (alt-ac), post-academic (post-ac), and adjunct communities on Twitter and elsewhere online. Two members of this community are the editors of this book, and others are contributors. I owe them all a large debt in compiling the manifesto and continue to owe them.

Some of the following five points will apply to you, and some won't. But, nevertheless, I continue to believe that it is time to shift our thinking.

1. Get Paid for Your Work

The first thing I told myself was this: Stop researching, writing, and editing for free. Get paid for your hard work. *You deserve it.*

I know getting started as a paid freelancer can be intimidating. Mulling over the pluses and minuses of this work can help you make better decisions, as Kelly J. Baker noted in her column on shifting her career to freelance writing, which I strongly recommend you read.[3] In fact, I recommend that you read everything you can about how to start making money for the hard work you do.

While you are taking good advice, please, do *not* listen to people who tell you flat out that you can't do it. There are a lot of naysayers out there. I don't know what their problem is. Just ignore them. I know it's hard. Don't listen to them.

The heart of the getting-paid point is this: *you are worth it.* And when you are an adjunct, a couple hundred bucks for a short piece in your area of expertise means groceries for your family for the month. Instead of taking on unpaid work in your department to catch someone's eye (maybe), earn some cash writing for a national audience and catch *everyone's* eye.

Speaking of that extra departmental labor: getting paid also means when your institution asks you to take on extra work, you ask for extra money. When someone *not* in your institution asks you to do labor in your area of expertise, bill them, politely.

You have a living to make.

There is one exception to the get-paid rule: love. If you truly love something, you can do it for free. But now and again you are required to re-read smart things people have written that shine light on how the "love" of teaching and research has been used to keep academics poor. Rebecca Schuman, Jacqui Shine, and William Pannapacker have all written well on this subject.[4] They'll remind you how love can trick us into doing things for free when we should be getting paid.

---

3. Kelly J. Baker, "To Write or Not to Write," *Chronicle Vitae*, September 9, 2014, https://chroniclevitae.com/news/694-to-write-or-not-to-write.

4. Rebecca Schuman, "Hanging Up on a Calling," *The Chronicle of Higher Education*, January 27, 2014, http://www.chronicle.com/article/Hanging-Up-on-a-Calling/144197; Jacqui Shine, "Love and Other Secondhand Emotions," *Chronicle Vitae*, February 3, 2014, https://chroniclevitae.com/news/309-love-and-other-secondhand-emotions; and William Pannapacker, "On Graduate School and 'Love,'" *The Chronicle of Higher Education*, October 1, 2013, http://www.chronicle.com/article/On-Graduate-SchoolLove/141965.

Whatever you do, don't get snookered by the "love" thing. We academics have been told for so long that money sullies the life of the mind. I call that malarkey. As Sarah Kendzior wrote in *Vitae*, "Should academics ever write for free? Maybe. Should academics write for free for a publisher that can afford to pay them? Never."[5]

2. Live in a Place You Love with the People You Love

Here's when love does matter. Academia teaches you to move away from the people and places you love in order to be successful. You have to be willing to move *anywhere* to find *any* job; otherwise you aren't dedicated enough. When I was on the job market fresh out of graduate school, I turned down shinier jobs all over the country for a contingent job. But I took that contingent job in order to be able to stay with my husband, to stay in a really nice place to live (Go Heels!), and also to stay where our parents live. I traded the tenure track for my humanity.

Unintentionally, I followed guideline number two on my list, here. The problem wasn't choosing my family over my career. The problem is that academia, as a career, has become so broken that we have to make this choice in the first place.

Forcing us to make the choice between our humanity and our careers is malarkey. Living away from the people we love is the opposite of living as a human being. If you have the choice, live with your family in a place where you enjoy living. Don't let anyone tell you that you are copping out by choosing your humanity over your academic credentials.

In a similar vein, if you want to have children, have children—create new small people to love. And if you don't, don't. And if you can't, you can have everyone read Elizabeth Keenan's column "The No-Baby Penalty" in *Vitae* so you don't have to explain your private business.[6]

3. They're Never Going to Let You in the Club

Stop hoping that the department where you are contingent is suddenly going to recognize that you are awesome (despite the fact that you are, indeed, awesome). So long as you hold out that glimmer of hope, they

5. Sarah Kendzior, "Should Academics Write for Free?" *Chronicle Vitae*, October 25, 2013, https://chroniclevitae.com/news/90-should-academics-write-for-free.

6. Elizabeth Keenan, "The No-Baby Penalty," *Chronicle Vitae*, June 19, 2014, https://chroniclevitae.com/news/570-the-no-baby-penalty.

hold all the power. You will keep taking on more free work, hoping that someone will tap you with a magic wand and make you a special fairy too.

Instead, step back and embrace freelancing. Now *you* hold the power. You no longer have only one path to success—the path through traditional academic streams. Now you have a universe of paths.

4. Stop Applying to Academic Jobs

This one might seem a little crazy, so bear with me.

The job market is too expensive—temporally, emotionally, and financially. The chances of the perfect job being right around the corner are slim to none. You're a freelancer now. So use the time and money you will save by not applying for jobs to start freelancing. Take a course on how to pitch ideas to writer's markets that pay, either through online courses or by hiring a successful freelancer friend to teach you. The course I took paid for itself within a week after I sold a story that I had workshopped during the course.

I know it's hard to let go of the dream of landing the perfect academic job. You might hear a story from a friend who knows someone whose cousin's mailman's niece finally landed a tenure-track position that was just right for her. You hear this story and think, *Just one more round of applications, and that will be me!*

It won't be you. I'm so sorry. You sound like someone who buys lottery tickets. Stop buying lottery tickets.

5. Remember That You Are Not Alone

Turning your academic knowledge and skills into cash is, itself, a skill. But there are people out there who can help you—hire a career coach who specializes in helping people transition out of the academy. And, from what I've encountered on social media, we all believe in each other. The most amazing thing of all is how much they all want to help you. It's miraculous. There will, of course, be jerks—the naysayers who will tell you that what you want to do is too hard or even impossible. Ignore them.

I don't live in the clouds. I know that most of us are struggling with money. I just got off of the couch where I was lying in a fear-ball, wondering how my family is going to survive now without my paycheck and benefits since I just took unpaid leave from what can only be described as an undesirable work environment. It's really hard not to look back. That's why I wrote this manifesto. I needed a mantra to keep me together. Now I'm sharing it with you.

But now that you have the manifesto, what do you do? Say you're still employed at a college, and you're not ready to leave yet (financially or emotionally). What do you do? I was in those shoes. That's where the exit plan comes in.

The University Is Just Another Client

Many times over the past few months, I've had some form of the conversation I'm about to describe with non-tenure-track (NTT) colleagues—and even some tenure-track (TT) ones.[7] I know I'm going to sound like I'm preaching with the fervor of the converted. But I haven't converted; I'm simply more aware now of university power dynamics (bless my former naïve heart) and how to use them, and I want my friends to share that awareness.

Here's a typical situation. I'm having coffee with a friend early on a Tuesday morning. She has been searching high and low for ways to break through the contingent ceiling. She is teaching on a nonrenewable contract at an institution and wants to find a way to encourage "them" to hire her on a more permanent basis when her contract expires.

With that goal in mind, she's taken on more service work, she's teaching an extra course (for no extra pay), *and* she's letting more students into the classes she already teaches—hoping that someone in a position of authority will recognize the awesome work she's doing. I was stunned by how much extra work she was describing. Since I tend toward bossiness, I consciously forced myself to just ask questions (and no, not *leading* questions) to get a full sense of what she was doing.

Finally, I asked, "Why are you doing all this extra work?"

And finally, she said something like, "I really want them to keep me on after my contract ends."

And there it was. The contingent faculty equivalent of writing a piece on spec. "On spec" is a term that journalists use to refer to editors asking newbie journalists to write pieces prior to being hired—because that's usually not how it goes. Usually, you pitch a piece, the editor accepts it, and

7. When I say non-tenure-track, I'm referring to all contingent employees of a university, including adjuncts, staff members in faculty-like roles (i.e., alternative-academic roles), and contingent instructors in full-time positions. Those different groups have different concerns. But for the purposes of this piece, I hope that all of them can derive usefulness from the ideas I'm about to share.

then you write it. Usually, you don't do the work without knowing whether you'll be paid or whether it will help your career.

Except what my friend described isn't like an article you write in your free time. She was talking about her whole career.

As a contingent faculty member, you work your whole career on spec. Every class you teach, every grant you write, every article you publish—they're all on spec, because you have no job security to back you up if a project doesn't pan out. You work and work, hoping some person in authority will give you (1) more money, (2) more job security, (3) more job respect, or some combination of (1), (2), and (3).

Spoiler alert: It doesn't work. As those of us who've been at this for a while know, giving administrators your work for free does not inspire them to reward you. More often it backfires and inspires administrators to turn your previously volunteered work into new job requirements. Suddenly what you did as a favor becomes a rigid job expectation.

Fortunately, I have a solution. It begins with a shift of mind-set—from that of employee to that of freelancer. As a freelancer, your institution is just one of your many clients. That means you need to spend your extra time and energy on projects that earn you both money and respect outside one particular institution.

You know who works on spec a lot? Freelancers. But they (usually) know how to do it while preserving their time, finances, and mental health.

NTTs are the freelancers of academia, and we need to start acting like it. Look at it this way: Your university has basically already said that you are a freelancer. You are already working job to job. That's what a year-to-year contract means. Or in the case of my friend, NTT means a terminal contract: she took a job with a client, and when that job ends, so does the client relationship.

Fine.

But if that is the case, then your institution will just be *one* of your many clients. Freelancers don't make a living hoping one client will keep hiring them over and over. They hustle and find other clients, too. We NTTs need to do the same. (And if you are a tenure-track professor reading this, and you have noticed that higher education might not be able to sustain you either, then I'm also talking to you. I firmly believe that it's time for *all* of us in higher education to diversify.) So instead of giving away your work for free, hoping for a reward that will likely never come, embrace the freelancer ethos.

Often when I suggest that we should apply this client-based strategy to academia, however, I get pushback. For some people, this strategy seems disloyal to their institution—as if you're cheating on your significant other. But you can only be loyal to a company that is loyal to you. And if you are NTT faculty, your institution is rarely going to be loyal to you.

In order to make time for yourself, you'll need to dial back the "adjunct heroics," as Rebecca Schuman puts it. That is exactly the advice that I would give my friend: Decline unpaid service work that won't be rewarded anyway. Keep office hours to the bare-bones requirement. Set limits on your letters of recommendations for students. And deflect all the guilt that others will probably lay on you—guilt from faculty, from students, and even from yourself.

It took me a while to adjust to the freelance academic mind-set. I really, really wanted to feel loyalty to the institution where I worked, and then the *next* institution where I worked. I wanted to find a home. But each time, the same thing happened: I was told, directly and indirectly, in large and small ways, that I did not belong because I was NTT. I felt betrayed and hurt. I cried, a lot. (You are probably very stoic and do not cry.) When these slights and put-downs and exploitations started happening at my second institution, I didn't feel like I'd been hoodwinked. I felt like I'd made the same dumb mistake twice, and I blamed myself.

The second time, I changed my mind-set completely. I couldn't quit outright—my family needed my salary. But I was ready to start planning an exit strategy. And I was ready to start making my life better right away. Enter the freelance mind-set. My institution, I decided, was just another client.

Say you've adjusted your mind-set. You're ready. Your institution is Client A. But it's time to look around for other clients, too. Who else is there? That might seem like the hard part, so bear with me for a minute.

Think about which of your skills are marketable. Sit down and write a list of every possible skill that you have. This is not the time to be humble. You might not know who to market your skills to, or how, but that's okay. You can start learning those things. You're an academic. You know how to research.

You need to transform your CV into a résumé—or various résumés for different types of work you might be interested in doing. When I did this myself, it was—and I'm not kidding—so much fun. I used Rachel Leventhal-Weiner's article on résumé writing for academics for guidance.[8] If you try

---

8. Rachel Leventhal-Weiner, "Don't Fear the Résumé," *Chronicle Vitae*, August 26, 2014, https://chroniclevitae.com/news/676-don-t-fear-the-resume.

to make your skills list and your résumé and have trouble—a totally un-derstandable problem, given how graduate programs are structured these days—hire a post-academic coach to help you figure out what you're good at that can earn you money.

Most important, at least for your mental health, recognize that you are not alone. Build a community, whether online or off, of others who are trying to do work similar to yours. That community will help you net-work into new opportunities and will reassure you when you start to doubt yourself. There are freelance networking communities that you can join. I subscribe to a newsletter called, unsurprisingly, "The Freelancer," which helped me learn about setting rates, dealing with clients, and more. And you can join the Freelancers Union to learn even more about the practical side of freelance life. They even have health and other kinds of insurance for their members.

Remember that moving into the mind-set of a Freelance Academic does not mean that you give up your job teaching on a campus. It just means that you approach your relationship with your institution differently. You no longer belong to them: *they belong to you.* Once that shift happens—and you'll know when it does—there's nothing more empowering.

In the months after I embraced being a Freelance Academic, I've been asked—and I've asked myself—a lot of complicated questions. Questions like: Does that term accurately describe what I'm trying to do? Can an ad-junct who is still in the academy be a freelance academic, too? And is that adjunct then an employee or a freelancer? I did some research to find out answers to those questions.

I received an email from a reader of my column once who told me that although she found my ideas about my career transition to be generally strong, she did not like the term "freelance academic" at all. Oddly enough, she had no problem with the "academic" part, but rather with "freelance." I know that reader meant well. Generally, her tone was supportive. But she spent an entire paragraph explaining how the word "freelance" "carries connotations of inferiority and lack of expertise or proficiency." It's a word people use, she wrote, "because they simply could not obtain a full-time paying gig."

Her recommended term? "Independent scholar." I've seen others use that phrase often enough, but it's not synonymous with "freelance aca-demic." Independent scholar does not at all describe the work that I do. For example, I do not conduct scholarship any more. I pretty much stopped writing scholarly work completely when I started writing for money. I have a few lingering scholarly articles coming out, but I'm not writing any new ones. (Unless you have a tenure-track position, the pay for publishing journal articles is terrible.) Thus, while "independent scholar" may describe very well what others do, it does not describe what freelance academics do.

But what about the second term in my chosen title, "academic"? In other debates over labels like "alternative academic" or "post-academic," I've heard other people express dislike of the use of "academic." Some of the arguments seem to suggest that when a person clings to the "academic" label, she is clinging to academia itself. Those arguments seemed persuasive to me, and they were made by people whose ideas I respect.

So I went to the dictionary. Oxford initially defines the adjective "academic" in this fashion: "of or relating to education and scholarship." I've already decided that scholarship, as such, is no longer for me.

But there's that other word—"education." I still do a lot with education. For example, I cover a higher-education beat in my freelance journalism (for money). I give talks that educate people about my areas of expertise, such as writing and disability studies. (I do that for money now, too, rather than just for a line on my CV.) I write textbooks to help people learn. I work as a developmental editor to help writers finish their manuscripts and get them out to publishers—educating my clients about writing.

I'm immersed in education, and my academic training has allowed me to do this work. It seems to me, then, that "freelance academic" is just the right term.

But What If I've Still Got a Foot inside the Academy?

What if you still work in higher education in some contingent position? What are the challenges in pursuing freelance academic work if you still count on a paycheck from a college or university?

There is one obvious barrier: Departments and institutions may frown on your nonacademic work. They don't want you distracted. They want you to focus on them, naturally. When I wrote my first book for money while I was a contingent academic, I was told that some members of my department were worried that my writing would "distract" me from teaching my many sections of composition—even though I was writing a textbook for the very subfield in which I taught.

But there are less obvious barriers as well.

"Megan" (a pseudonym) adjuncts at two different institutions to make ends meet. Despite her multi-campus teaching, she still ends up with a "below-poverty-level adjunct salary." In an interview, she pointed out "one humongous issue" that "has to do with how institutions hire adjuncts and how [adjuncts] are taxed." Megan insists—and I concur—that adjuncts "should be hired as regular freelancers, so that we can actually deduct expenses, such as partial use of home as office, since we are never given an individual office."

Her exasperation is plain in her tone: "It is completely absurd that we are taxed like regular employees, but have absolutely no benefits, and then we cannot even deduct the costs of our own work. This is really too much."

It's true. Freelancers typically lack the security of regular employment, but they have the benefit of deducting lots of expenses: pens, paper, laptops, printers, home office space. Those are all things that adjuncts use to do their jobs.

When you freelance outside the academy, you are doing external work that is *not* taxed like your work at your institution. The income from that external work is called "1099 income," and you would deduct your freelance expenses from that income. However, finding the time to pursue 1099 income while adjuncting full-time on two campuses can be next to impossible. Most adjuncts are often just too busy.

Would a better solution be to classify adjuncts as 1099 independent contractors rather than as W-2 employees? Is such a thing even possible?

To answer my questions, I talked with a tax law professor at the University of North Carolina School of Law, Kathleen DeLaney Thomas. My first question: Under tax law, can adjuncts be classified as 1099 employees? That's unlikely, according to Thomas. "The IRS has taken the position in most cases that adjunct professors are employees," she said, "and courts have generally agreed." That classification really isn't up to the employer. "In fact," Thomas said, "it can be more expensive for the employer to hire [a W-2] employee because the employer is then responsible for FICA taxes, federal and state unemployment, and possibly worker's comp," whereas employers "can avoid payroll taxes and withholding obligations for independent contractors, who have to pay self-employment taxes on their own."

But what about the classic "freeway flier"—the adjunct who teaches on multiple campuses and lacks almost any institutional support? While "the 'freeway flier' is a sympathetic case," Thomas said, "unfortunately for those professors, the precedent for independent contractor status is not good." She pointed to a US Tax Court decision that "held that an adjunct college professor teaching online courses was an employee, notwithstanding the fact that the professor provided his own computer and Internet connection and had no office at the school."[9]

9. See US Tax Court, *Schramm v. Commissioner*, T.C. Memo, 2011-212 (August 30, 2011).

In the end—however much adjuncts and other contingent faculty may feel like they aren't treated as employees—in the eyes of the IRS, they will be classified as employees for the foreseeable future. Our university teaching will not count as freelance work, which means we won't be able to deduct any expenses related to that work.

I'm sorry to be the bearer of that bad news, but Megan's question was an important one. Those of us who are embracing the freelancer ethos need to understand the structural limitations on our freelancing work.

But we can still find freelancing work outside our institutions. The university is, after all, just another client. So you want to deduct your laptop, pens, printer, paper, and all of your other purchases on your taxes? Great— you can. Earn some side money through your other freelancing work. If you can, turn down that fourth or fifth adjunct course, and use that time to earn money through actual freelance gigs instead. Educate yourself about IRS rules. (It's not that complicated, I promise, and there are great resources out there. The Freelancers Union has an online booklet called the "First-Time Freelancer's Guide to Taxes" that I highly recommend.)

I know that everything I've recommended requires risk taking on your part. I've taken those risks, too, and they're scary. One day I walked away from relatively secure employment—as secure as an NTT can get, really, because the working conditions were just too hard. That was one of the scariest days of my life. I didn't know how we were going to keep our house. I'd written a plan of how we were going to live on one salary, and the plan was severe.

But then this magical thing happened. Although the first year was a little lean, I started making money. I had all this time to try new things, and some started to pan out. I realized that no one knows how to hustle like a person who taught first-year writing on multiple campuses in multiple cities while pregnant. I just needed to redirect that hustle in a way that benefited a career that I controlled, rather than benefiting institutions that didn't care about me at all.

You can do it too. You can take all your energy and drive and succeed in whatever path you choose, whether that path is remaining in academia and freelancing on the side, or working part-time in academia and freelancing part-time, or leaving academia completely as I did and finding an entirely new career that makes you so much happier. Just remember: Get paid for your work. Live in a place you love with the people you love. They're never going to let you in the club. Stop applying to academic jobs. And most importantly, you are not alone.

9

Faculty Development

The (Unnecessarily) Long and Winding Road

LEE SKALLERUP BESSETTE

When I decided to do my PhD, it was primarily because I wanted to teach. The thought of teaching college students my first (academic) love, Canadian literature, while also studying it full-time was too seductive a proposition for me to pass up. I had been coaching swimming since I was fifteen and teaching ESL for a couple of summers. Additionally, many claimed that I was a "natural" teacher. In other words, I spoke well in front of crowds and had enough personality to hold people's attention, as well as a deep passion for and commitment to whatever I was talking about, which also came through when I taught. The decision to do a PhD was a no-brainer for me.

I did everything "right" to become a "successful" academic: I chose a prestigious program, I presented at conferences, I published articles, and I received fellowships. I taught some classes as an adjunct, but only to gain a wider variety of teaching experiences, working at a Hispanic-serving institution. When the time came, I applied widely, highlighting my teaching experience and work with nontraditional students. And I was rewarded: in 2008, I started a tenure-track job at a historically Black college and university.

I also did everything "wrong"; little did I know that at the end of the day, my focus on teaching instead of research was in fact a liability for traditional academic success. The academy primarily rewards research productivity, not teaching excellence. I also got married and started a family, and I didn't marry just anyone; no, I married a fellow academic. We were the classic two-body problem. I had a tenure-track job, and I gave it up. I gave it up so my husband could accept a better tenure-track job. I gave up my tenure-track job because I had two kids under the age of two and didn't want to live apart from my spouse.

I found myself in an isolated rural community with two young children and a husband on the tenure track. I lived an increasingly common academic storyline: an unsatisfying contingent position with no paths forward for my professional career. I was told by my colleagues, both on and off the tenure track, that I should be grateful for the contingent position. Wasn't I "lucky" to be able to still teach, at the same institution as my husband no less, and be "free" from the responsibilities of the tenure track, as well as free to be a good wife and mother? We lived in a very conservative part of the country; many of my colleagues still believed that being a faculty wife was a noble aspiration. Others saw the fact that I had given up a tenure-track job as proof positive that I wasn't serious about being an academic and so had no right to complain about my situation.

I was also excluded from university life. I had zero say in governance or curricular decisions. A heavy course load meant that it became increasingly difficult to do the research I also loved. Lack of institutional support made it almost impossible to attend conferences. Giving up a tenure-track job for a contingent position also became a black mark on my CV. Giving up a tenure-track position one year in signaled to hiring committees either that I wasn't serious or couldn't cut it. It was made very clear to me on my own campus that I had become a disposable academic and was largely treated accordingly. Living in a small rural town wary of outsiders meant that I also didn't have any community outside the institution.

The breaking point, for me, came when a colleague of mine who was in a similar position, having come to that same institution as the wife of a tenure-track academic and having remained in a contingent position the rest of her career, announced her retirement. I had just turned thirty-five the day before, and the thought of spending the next thirty years in that same position, teaching the same classes, for (most likely) the same salary was too much for me to bear. With the lack of support, the lack of recognition, and the lack of resources, I couldn't do it anymore.

I wish it hadn't taken a moment like that to set me on a different, and ultimately more professionally fulfilling, path. I found myself at my lowest point; I wish it had happened earlier in my career, when I wasn't broken down.

During my first year, I started blogging and got on Twitter, in part as a way to stay sane, to connect, and to find community. The short, alternate version of this story is that I would not be where I am today if not for my blog and for Twitter. I found communities of scholars, of activists, of people who were generous and welcoming and who valued what I had to offer. I was empowered to write about teaching and contingent faculty issues and digital humanities (among other things) on my blog. I cofounded a Twitter chat for those of us teaching first-year composition. I got involved with contingent faculty organizations. All this led to a writing gig with the University of Venus and then the blog *Ready Writing* at *Inside Higher Ed*. And then writing for *Women in Higher Education*. And then *Educating Modern Learners*. And then *ProfHacker*. It led to invitations to speak at conferences and be on panels at my disciplinary conferences. It's where I learned about the possibility of faculty development.

I wish that I'd known people like the ones I found on Twitter while I was in graduate school (to be fair, one of the people who set me on the faculty development path was a colleague from graduate school who was a few years ahead of me). I wish that I had known that something like alternative-academic (alt-ac) careers existed and were fulfilling and challenging and exciting and *worthy* of my time and attention while I was setting my career goals in graduate school. I wish I hadn't been told to give up writing on the Internet back when I started my PhD because no one would take me seriously as an academic otherwise. I wish I had had people around me who empowered me and encouraged me, and not just in the narrow ways deemed necessary to be successful in academia, but in all the ways I could flourish.

Looking back, faculty development makes more sense for me, professionally, than a tenure-track job ever did. But I didn't even know a job like the one I now have existed when I started my PhD. How could I know that it would be a fit for me? I hope that some of you can avoid unnecessary years as an adjunct to come to see faculty development as a rewarding and fulfilling career. Faculty development is an ideal alt-ac career for those who are passionate and knowledgeable about pedagogy and technology. Yet as it was to me, the field can largely be invisible for PhD students and adjuncts.

What Is Faculty Development?

There isn't one agreed-upon job title for what it is that I do, which is to help faculty be better teachers and pedagogues. This lack of a particular job title is one of the reasons that my career path took a long time and remains obscured for many. Within faculty development, we work in teaching and learning centers as well as academic technology units, and we can also be called faculty developers, educational developers, faculty instructional consultants, instructional technology specialists, academic technologists, instructional designers, e-learning specialists. The list is extensive.[1]

Ultimately, my job involves working with faculty to improve their classrooms, teaching, assignments, assessments, syllabi, learning outcomes, and curricula. I have also worked at the administrative level to implement college- or campus-wide curricular reform. I specialize in the integration of digital tools and approaches into teaching and learning, but I also work on active learning, meaningful assessments, and online learning design. As I explain to my kids, I help the professors be better teachers, especially with technology.

My work in faculty development started with my own frustration with my teaching. I knew I wasn't doing a good enough job with and for my students, and so began a long journey to improve my teaching. There was little support for me at my own institution, but I had recently discovered Twitter and began connecting with other educators through the medium, specifically via Twitter chats and then through their blogs. I began blogging about my own experiments in pedagogy, particularly in engaging my students with and through technology. I also became interested in digital humanities, which allowed me to further expand my digital and scholarly skills and techniques.[2]

I began to share my experiences through social media and blogging, as well as by providing peer-driven, project-based learning to a wider audience through online and face-to-face workshops. I made sure that I shared resources I developed and experiences I had gained openly through Twitter and my blog. My public, experimental pedagogy might not have been well-received at my home institution, but it was being promoted and, dare I say, celebrated within the wider community.

Teaching had always mattered to me; pedagogy had always mattered to me. I cared deeply about the students in front of me, about their learning experience. How we teach *matters*. But I also recognized early on in my education that as important as the classroom experience was for students, any real improvement to the educational experience had to be implemented on

1. For more information on the definition of educational development, see "What Is Educational Development?" POD Network, June 2016, http://podnet work.org/about-us/what-is-educational-development/.

2. The debate about what is digital humanities is extensive, but this definition from Wikipedia will suffice for the purpose of this chapter: "An area of scholarly activity at the intersection of computing or digital technologies and the disciplines of the humanities, it includes the systematic use of digital resources in the humanities, as well as the reflection on their application."

a larger, systemic level. I had always gotten involved in any way that I could, from facilitating a discussion between faculty and my fellow undergraduates about programmatic reform, to becoming Graduate Student Association president during my PhD, to being involved nationally in advocacy for adjunct faculty. I was not going to change the system, however, from my position as contingent faculty. We are by our very nature excluded from the governance and running of the university.

So when I announced I was done with trying to get a tenure-track job and done with being a contingent faculty member, a former colleague from graduate school suggested I look into faculty development. I checked all the boxes: I had experience as a faculty member, I was experienced at working with faculty on incorporating technology into their pedagogy, I had published in and presented at a number of prestigious outlets, and I had shown myself willing and able to try new approaches effectively, not to mention a willingness to engage in larger conversations around systemic reform. And when I said, "yes, this sounds perfect for me," a number of other people in my network reached out to help me get started. I said it earlier, but I want to reiterate, if it were not for the network that I developed through blogging and on Twitter, I would not have been as successful in transitioning into faculty development.

Getting Started

The best place to get started learning about faculty development is through the Professional Organizational Development Network at podnet work.org. One of the first things I did was to sign up for their listserv and go through the archive looking through past job ads that were shared on the list. That provides a really good idea of the breadth of jobs available, as well as the skills and experiences employers are seeking.

The POD Network website also has a really fantastic page for getting started in faculty development.[3] That page recommends that you have the following skills and aptitudes:

- Knowledge of group dynamics, information technology, higher education, and the literature on teaching and learning (e.g., curriculum development, active and engaged learning, inclusive teaching).

3. "Getting Started in an Educational Development Career," POD Network, http://podnetwork.org/about-us/what-is-educational-development/getting -started-in-an-educational-development-career/.

- Skills such as how to facilitate workshops, do research or program evaluations, engage in event planning and project management, teach in large and small groups, and communicate effectively with diverse academic audiences. Interpersonal capacities are particularly important, such as the ability to mentor and coach others, mediate conflicts, and facilitate group discussions and meetings.
- Attitudes such as patience, persistence, comfort with technology and collaborative work, and openness to feedback, reflective practice, and interdisciplinarity.

I had a great deal of classroom experience, an aptitude and openness to using and learning various technologies (what we would consider educational technologies, and others), experience giving workshops both online and face-to-face, and a proven record of reflective practice through my blog. I had planned a number of conferences and other events as a graduate student and a number of The Humanities and Technology Camps (THAT-Camps) as a contingent faculty member. One area in which I was lacking, at least more recently, was in the area of collaboration; there just aren't many opportunities to collaborate when you're a contingent faculty member. But I had a number of collaborations with colleagues scattered across the country (and even the world) through social media.

I had just about all the pieces in place, experiences that looked random and piecemeal when trying for a traditional academic position but fit together perfectly when I began to reframe myself as a faculty developer. I had previously done a very traditional skills (and experiences) inventory for myself and realized that the breadth of my formal and informal experiences were a strength; I just had to find the right career for them.[4]

The POD Network page also provides four steps to follow to prepare for a career in faculty development (here abbreviated as ED for educational development). Here they are, abridged, with my own thoughts on the steps:

1. FIND THE CENTER FOR TEACHING AND LEARNING (CTL) NEAREST TO YOU. INFORMATIONAL INTERVIEWS WITH STAFF HELP ESTABLISH THE RANGE OF WAYS CENTERS CAN ENGAGE GRADUATE STUDENTS AND POSTDOCS AND OFFER USEFUL CONVERSATIONS FOR EXPLORING

4. "Skills Inventory," *Inside Higher Ed*, November 19, 2014, https://www.inside highered.com/blogs/college-ready-writing/skills-inventory.

AN ED JOB SEARCH. MANY CENTERS ALSO OFFER PAID OPPORTUNITIES, SUCH AS INTERNSHIPS AND GRADUATE TEACHING CONSULTANT PROGRAMS. WHILE PARTICIPATING IN A CTL'S WORKSHOPS AND PROGRAMS IS HELPFUL, SERVING AS A FACILITATOR OR CO-FACILITATOR IS MORE VALUABLE EXPERIENCE IN THE ED JOB MARKET.

I cannot stress this enough—find your teaching and learning center as soon as possible and connect with them, and this includes places that support digital or online learning. Take workshops, offer workshops, be a part of faculty learning communities (FLCs), and offer to lead them. Partner with them on doing research, as well as with your students. And if your institution doesn't have a center, then start your own FLC or informal workshop series. Find other faculty and/or graduate students who are interested in improving their teaching, and see if you can have monthly meetings at least. Be proactive and connect with the community on your campus as soon as you can. If your institution doesn't have a teaching and learning center, see if there is one at a school nearby or participate in virtual workshops, Twitter chats, and events.

2. TAILOR YOUR JOB SEARCH MATERIALS TO ED SEARCHES, SUCH AS BY HIGHLIGHTING THE RATIONALE FOR AN ED SEARCH AND WAYS IN WHICH YOU HAVE DEVELOPED SKILL SETS IN SOME OF THE COMPETENCIES NAMED ABOVE. IT ALSO IS USEFUL TO DEVELOP AN ED PHILOSOPHY STATEMENT OR PORTFOLIO.

You still get to write a longer narrative for your job letter, and your CV can remain a long-form document, but the focus shifts to your work related to teaching and learning. Unlearn your traditional academic narrative and learn to retell it for faculty development. This was one of the biggest challenges for me, but also the most rewarding part of the entire process (other than getting my first job). Reading sample letters from successful colleagues was probably the single most helpful thing I did. As a result, I was able to bring together all my varied and seemingly unconnected experiences into a cohesive narrative that made me sound like an ideal candidate for faculty development positions, particularly those that used and taught technology.

And, the ED philosophy statement is a lot like your teaching philosophy statement and can act as an important starting point for reimagining who you will be as a faculty developer, as opposed to a teacher. Think of it this way: how will you approach teaching the teachers, and collaborating with them and the administration to improve teaching and learning?

3. LINK INTO COMMUNITIES OF PRACTICE, BOTH ONLINE (E.G., THE POD NETWORK DISCUSSION GROUP) AND IN PERSON AT ANNUAL MEETINGS, SUCH AS THE POD NETWORK CONFERENCE, LILLY CONFERENCES, AND ISSOTL.

Yes. This. But I would expand the scope of this advice, big time. The list of professional conferences, communities, and forums that can benefit you and help you be a successful faculty developer are much more extensive than this list. Newer online publications such as *Hybrid Pedagogy* and the *Journal of Interactive Technology and Pedagogy* are pushing the conversation on teaching and learning. The Humanities, Arts, Science, and Technology Alliance and Collaboratory (HASTAC) network and blog also provide a wealth of resources and a large community. Most of the authors on these sites are also on Twitter, which is still my go-to network for larger conversations on teaching, learning, and technology. THATCamps are also useful (and cheaper) alternatives to connecting with people interested in teaching, learning, and technology. I keep including technology because increasingly, you cannot have a conversation about teaching and learning without including technology. If I have one critique of POD, it is that they have been slow to embrace these conversations. Think about what you are interested in and passionate about, and explore that area, be it assessment, Open Education Resources, learning spaces, or something else.

The POD Network discussion group is the primary way that jobs in faculty development are shared, so it provides a great resource for figuring out what kind of faculty development job is right for you. Read the job ads and see what skills you already possess and brainstorm ways you can gain the experience or expertise you lack. Ask questions. Read. Listen. And contribute to the conversation yourself by writing. Heck, push the conversation in new directions.

4. EXPLORE RESOURCES SUCH AS *THE GUIDE TO FACULTY DEVELOPMENT* (GILLESPIE AND ROBERTSON, 2007), *PRACTICALLY SPEAKING* (BRINKO, 2012), OR *TO IMPROVE THE ACADEMY*, WHICH DISCUSS APPROACHES AND PROFICIENCIES THAT EDUCATIONAL DEVELOPERS EMPLOY IN THEIR WORK. ADDITIONALLY, IT IS HELPFUL TO LEARN ABOUT TRENDS IN HIGHER EDUCATION THROUGH

RESOURCES SUCH AS *INSIDE HIGHER ED, CHRONICLE OF HIGHER EDUCATION,* AND *CHANGE MAGAZINE.*

See my advice under number 3.

The problem I have with number 4 is that this list of resources to read is short and traditionalist. I truly believe that if we are to have any sort of lasting impact on higher education and to see the kind of change that will matter in the long run, we need to embrace the full meaning of our "alternative-academic" moniker. We need to rethink and reshape how we talk about teaching and learning and technology, using those tools and techniques we want our faculty and our institutions to embrace. The resources in number 4, however, are invaluable for learning what I call "the canon" for faculty development, allowing you to understand the terms and shared language, as well as the dominant narrative of faculty development as a profession.

We are academics, still and always, but in our alternative roles we do not have to adhere to the traditional forms and expectations imposed on the tenure-track researcher. We should be learning from newer disciplines like women's studies, ethnic studies, library studies (which is not new but often overlooked), and digital humanities, as well as our own "home" disciplines and the scholarship of teaching and learning (SOTL). We do need to be paying attention, but if all we read are the usual suspects, we risk recreating the same exclusionary power structures that led many of us to seek alt-ac jobs in the first place.

It's no secret that faculty development has a diversity problem, like most areas of higher education. It also shares some of the challenges faced by librarians because faculty development is seen, increasingly, as "feminized" labor. We are also understood, often, as a "service" shop, a glorified help desk. There is much work to be done still in educating the larger institution about our role and what we do. It can be a double-edged sword—our PhD or advanced degrees give us legitimacy in the eyes of the faculty we work with, but then often our expertise is either not valued or dismissed.

By insisting on and opening up our scholarship, our approaches, our view, we can hopefully welcome new and important voices into these pivotal roles within our institutions. We need to foster collaborative relationships with places like the library, IT, and other "support" units on campus. Ultimately, we all have the same goal, which is to improve students' learning and the student experience. Faculty development and centers for teaching and learning can be important sites of collaborating for change. We need to value and celebrate the kind of scholarship, of collaborations, of work that traditionally the academy has not.

Final Thoughts

The faculty development job market is not like the academic job market insofar as there is not only one hiring season. In fact, you could say that there are three "waves" of hiring—the ones that take place early in the academic year, the ones that take place during the second semester, and then ones that come open over the summer. The interview process itself is similar: a video conference round and then an on-campus round. The timeline is usually much quicker than a traditional academic job as well.

There can be numerous directions forward in faculty development, from an entry-level position to assistant or associate director to director-level positions. One of the challenges is that higher-level positions are often reserved for faculty with tenure, but as there are less and less of those, these positions may start becoming available to exclusively alt-ac people. It's not perfect, but it's been largely fulfilling for me so far. There are often opportunities to teach, and in fact in some places it is required in order to be able to say that we are practicing what we preach.

I was extraordinarily lucky to get my first job in faculty development. I have written elsewhere that it took 99,000 tweets to get me that first job. It was a tweet I just shot off about moving and needing a job that led to the job itself, which I had unsuccessfully applied for during the previous academic year. That shows people out there are willing to support you and take a chance on you if you let them.

One final admission: there are days when I still feel like a failed academic rather than a successful faculty developer. There are days when I'm not sure I still want to stay in academia. The inequalities and injustices of academia are still frustratingly present; the narrative of academic success and failure stubbornly persists. I am still an academic; I still teach; I am employed and (relatively) fairly compensated for my work. But there are still days when I wonder if it's enough.

And that's okay.

I still believe that this is a path, one with value, one that is rewarding, one that can transform and be transformative.

10

You Never Know

From Professor to (UX) Professional

ABBY BAJUNIEMI

I started out my graduate program thinking I'd be a professor. (Shocking, I know.) I labored under that idea my entire graduate career, even as my relationship with my adviser deteriorated. Yet I soured on the idea of a tenure-track job. I wanted to flee academia—fast. Here's the tl;dr version: my adviser became abusive and judgmental when I suggested I wouldn't uproot my life for a professorship.

Toward the end of my program, I landed a job as a visiting assistant professor at a local small liberal arts college. I was happy there. I taught two courses per semester and was paid more than I was making as a graduate student and more than most adjuncts made—and I had benefits. I had great colleagues and students. I also taught in my field (linguistics) occasionally. I was told "You never know" about full-time positions, so I kept accepting teaching assignments, hoping I'd land one. I was treated so well that I thought I was the exception to the rule.

Then a full-time, non-tenure-track colleague left. Instead of offering her position to me or the other adjunct, they chose to do a national search. I thought, "Okay, this isn't gonna happen. As much as I love my job, it's not sustainable and not a real career." This pushed me into a nonacademic job search.

Because I thought I'd be a professor, I'd never sought out alternative careers or connections. Now I want to give hope to those who are feeling that it's too late to transition out of academia. It will be harder, for sure, but it's not too late.

Reimagining My Career

I felt that I was already behind. In summer 2015, I began searching for stories of nonacademic PhDs to see what careers they were in. There's a lot of information on reframing the skills gained as a PhD, from The Professor Is In to Jobs on Toast and Versatile PhD. Although much of the advice was geared toward STEM PhDs, I learned some things: teaching can be reframed as workshop facilitation, papers and research work translated to project management skills, and classroom management becomes leadership skills. All those conferences? Public speaking and thought leadership.

There are many other ways to reframe your skills, and there are lots of resources to help you. What I lacked was concrete examples of linguists succeeding outside academia. I wanted to see specific examples, since we don't have an "industry," as STEM PhDs do. I discovered Career Linguist, where I read about a linguist who works as a researcher in user experience (UX). Intrigued, I immediately searched for information on UX. I also did courses on Lynda.com—if it was out there, I consumed it.[1] I discovered that an applied linguist like me is suited to UX because we work with language users, document what they do with language, and provide interpretations of this use. I also learned that someone who can design and carry out field research is valuable to UX.

I then checked whether I knew anyone who worked in UX. Networking is crucial. You'll need to rely on your connections to get jobs because most people are not familiar with the benefits of hiring PhDs and might dismiss you as being overeducated or overqualified. Luckily, my mother is a keen businesswoman; she put me in contact with the principal and CEO of a research/design firm. A family friend sent an email to her to introduce me, and we set up a phone call. She asked me about what I'd done in my graduate program and as a visiting assistant professor. She then asked if I had any business experience and why I thought I would be good at UX.

I stumbled a little in my description of my work and processes. Much like learning a new language, changing your vocabulary about what you do and who you are to sound less academic can be awkward. I did well enough, though, that she told me I sounded like a great fit for user research and that I needed a website immediately that included any previous work that I could finagle into UX deliverables or that showcased studies of the type of work I could provide to a UX team. She then introduced me to the director of her local office to discuss working together in the future. She

1. Check whether your university has access to Lynda.com courses. Mine did.

also suggested local UX Meetup groups that I should look into in addition to the User Experience Professionals Association's (UXPA's) local chapter.

Armed with her confidence in me and ideas about more things to do (I'm like a corgi—I need a job), I signed up for the local UXPA chapter and local Meetup groups. The first UXPA meeting was their free summer social, where I met tons of amazing people. But I didn't have business cards and I am extremely shy, so I didn't leave with good contacts. It felt like being a grad student at a conference: too nervous to talk to anyone with any amount of power, you hang out with other grad students, which gets you nothing on the job market.

I did a lot of listening, which ultimately helped me frame myself as a UX professional. I did meetups and UXPA events for a while, but I never got anywhere because I wasn't meeting decision-makers. The people with the hiring power tend not to go to these things because they are very busy. This makes sense in hindsight.

The presentations were interesting, and I was learning a lot, but I was getting frustrated by my looming unemployment and lack of leads. After a hectic semester in spring 2016, I asked a friend if she knew anyone she could introduce me to. Her reply: "Yep. Get ready."

So I did.

I wrote up a blurb about myself, and I had almost ten coffees/phone calls lined up within a week. When you write about yourself, include a few basic things:

- who you are and what you're doing
- what you're looking for
- what kinds of people you are looking to connect with and why.

It shouldn't be long. Think about what you want strangers (who could help you get a job) to know about you.

My first draft was terrible and way too academic. No one cares about your academic stuff. They care about your skills and what you bring to an organization. I drafted my blurb and then had someone I trusted read it and tell me when I sounded too academic.

The finished blurb I sent out still wasn't great, but now I'm much better at it. It takes some time to get your message right, and you will need help to make it clear and direct. No wordy academese. Think plain language. After I did that, I learned two things: (1) you never know who knows whom and (2) people in general want to help other people, so ask everyone, even casual acquaintances, if they or their friends can introduce you to someone.

Through one of these ten contacts, I was introduced to another principal and CEO of a research/design firm, who told me, "Don't let the people who don't get you frustrate you. People are afraid of education, and they are afraid of women with brains." I experienced some of this. I had my résumé dismissed out of hand because the recipient did not understand what I had to offer. My lack of distinct business experience trumped all the awesome skills I could bring to the job. Some people balked openly at my PhD.

She also told me that this is a long game, and it could take months for something to pop. In the meantime, she advised me to keep connecting with others and putting myself out there. I've met amazing people who think my research is cool and who see my value. Each time I met with a new person, I left with a new perspective and ways to think about myself, my work, and my potential contributions. This last CEO told me how to lay out my experience on my résumé and helped me tweak some wording to get more attention. For example, I had been calling myself a "UX Researcher," but she said that "Design Researcher" is the sexy term right now. I wouldn't have known about this trend had she not told me. Another woman I met helped me reimagine myself as a senior researcher (after seven years, you can call yourself that!), as someone who needs to position herself for higher-level roles, and that this move is a career pivot rather than a change. Another reinforced the idea that I need to sell myself as a senior researcher, saying, "You've got serious research chops—don't discount that! We need you."

All this networking paid off. I was put in touch with a recruiter, and he secured a contract at a large international corporation at a rate that was almost $40,000 more a year than I made as an adjunct.

You will occasionally be asked your desired salary range when talking to people. It's helpful to Google average salaries in the field in your desired location. Sites like Glassdoor can also provide a range. Then once you know the range, do what Meghan McInerny tweeted on October 14, 2015: "My advice on salary negotiation for women. Ask for it, and then earn it. Not the other way around."[2]

You may not get it, but it shows that you value yourself and your knowledge. If someone insists on knowing your current salary, hold strong and do not divulge it.[3] For my first position, I was told by a trusted director of a UX

2. COO of Clockwork (www.clockwork.com) and a badass woman I admire greatly. You can find the tweet at https://twitter.com/irishgirl/status/654139804607602688.

3. *Note*: This is now illegal in some states, so they shouldn't be asking you this in the first place! See "California Commission on Women: Pay Equity Task Force,"

agency that I should be pulling in "at least" $50 per hour as a consultant. For a full-time salaried position, it would be less, but he told me I shouldn't be accepting anything less than $65,000 a year. When that first position fell into my lap, the recruiter offered me $60,000. I said, "I'm looking to be closer to $67,000." He came back quickly, saying the manager accepted that rate. It was the most money I had ever been offered. I almost fell out of my chair.

For my second industry position, I was asked several times by the "talent acquisition" person during the interview phase about my current salary. Because I wanted to increase my rate, I always responded with, "I am looking to land closer to $80,000." He kept asking me, and I stayed firm with my response. When I got the offer and he asked me my salary requirement, I responded as I always did: "I am looking to land closer to $80,000," and he said, "How about $75,000?" I was happy with that number given the benefits, so I accepted. That doesn't mean that that number didn't "make me sweaty." I was so anxious about this negotiation, having never asked for this amount of money before. I learned that when they really want you, they will do what they can to get you. Don't be afraid to ask for what you deserve to make.

Networking 101

So remember that first job I got? I didn't like it. This will happen. The job wasn't what was advertised to me, nor was it a good fit. I was hired on to a customer experience (CX) team, and my title was CX Insights Analyst. I was told it was "UX-adjacent," and I would be doing similar work. Yet I spent my days reading marketing reports and pulling "market insights" for the strategy team. It was like my PhD preliminary exams all over again, but on a topic I did not give one tiny shit about.

I was promised I'd get to facilitate workshops and then "maybe" I'd get to do design research in the future, "when the team is more stable." This felt like my old program dangling a carrot on a stick in front of me. "You never know." But I knew.

The people there were fantastic. I was good at what they asked me to do, but you have to like the work you're doing, not just your colleagues. I did what jobseekers often do: I reached out to my network again. Because I played the long game, I maintained my connections and made new ones, which helped when I realized I needed a change.

She Negotiates, She Succeeds, 2016, http://www.shenegotiates.com/california-pay-equity-task-force.

Before I go into what I did specifically, I'll share my experience networking. I know that word might sound ugly or feel manipulative. Although academics frequently say you shouldn't have to do it because your work will speak for you, *they all do it, too.* Outside academia, everyone does it, and everyone expects it. It's mutual. You will one day be in a position to help others, and the expectation is that you will. People are generally eager to help, and they remember what it's like to be new.

1. DON'T BE AFRAID TO ASK YOUR FAMILY, FRIENDS, AND ACQUAINTANCES IF THEY KNOW ANYONE IN X FIELD.

Someone you know likely has an impressive network. I asked a woman I knew through my kettlebell class, I asked my mom for introductions, and I talked to friends and spouses of friends. I know some people who threw out a "Hey, does anyone know anyone in X field?" on Twitter and Facebook. It's possible to get a lot of introductions this way.

2. PERSONAL INTRODUCTIONS ARE FAR MORE EFFECTIVE THAN BLIND CALLS OR EMAILS.

People are busy. Sometimes they honestly don't have time to work in a personal introduction to their network. Blindly contacting people can be off-putting or easy for recipients to ignore, especially if they are busy. There are exceptions to the rule—I have one new industry friend whom I emailed (with the referrer's name) who responded and was amazing.

As often as you can, ask for and kindly insist upon a personal introduction. As a friend said to me, "Anyone that X says I should meet, I definitely want to meet." You can and ought to ask someone you're meeting if they know of anyone else you should meet or if they have any ideas about people you should be connecting with. If they say yes, ask if they'll introduce you. Most of the time, they will be delighted. If they say they will give you the email of someone you should meet, ask them if you can use their name in the cold email.

3. IF YOU DON'T HAVE LUCK WITH YOUR PERSONAL NETWORK, LOOK FOR MEETUP GROUPS OR PROFESSIONAL GROUPS IN THE FIELD.

Pretty self-explanatory. If you can't find any appropriate groups on Meetup, then ask about professional groups and working groups for your new field when you're at networking meetings with industry professionals. If it's invitation-only, ask for an invitation.

4. LEARN THE LANGUAGE.

It's important to figure out how to translate your experience and skills into the terminology of a new field. For example, "ethnography" becomes "contextual inquiry" or "field studies" in UX; "localization" is targeting language/content toward a particular group (or "segment"). Going to industry functions and networking will help you learn this new language. Some of your new contacts may help you with this if you bring along a résumé.

5. KNOW YOUR VALUE.

You've done a PhD. You have mad researching skills. Don't undervalue yourself. Networking will be especially important for you since the HR filters won't know what to do with you.

6. AIM FOR MANAGERIAL OR HIGHER-LEVEL PEOPLE.

These are the people with the power to hire you. It's not bad to meet people who are at your level or slightly above, especially as you're learning about the field, but the big hitters can help you get insights into getting hired. It's also easier to get access to C-suite (CEO, COO, CTO, CIO, etc.) people at small companies than large ones, but you can still connect with managers and/or directors at larger companies. They're usually busy, though. Respecting their time is especially important. Be open to phone calls. Sometimes, that's all they will have time for, and that's okay.

7. CONTINUE TO MAKE CONNECTIONS (AND FOLLOW UP!) AND THEN PAY IT FORWARD WHEN YOU ARE SUCCESSFULLY EMPLOYED.

My general rules of networking: (1) be polite and respect their time; (2) tell them why you want to meet with them.

Offer some meeting options they can choose. They are busy. You also want to offer to meet at a location that is most convenient for them. That means you may have to drive a ways. Always thank them for taking the time to meet you. After meeting them, send a thank-you note within twenty-four hours and a reminder of anything they said they could do for you or you for them (i.e., introductions to the next person). *Never* say, "I'd like to pick your brain." This sounds skeevy and might remind them of cold-callers who just want free advice. Instead, ask to learn about the person. If you don't get a reply within one week, send another email a week later. Do not send more than two to three emails. Above that number, you become annoying.

Here are some examples. First, after an introduction:

Dear Sarah,

Thank you so much for agreeing to meet with me. I'm excited to learn more about you and your work on [company]'s UX team. I'd love to set up a coffee with you to chat! If mornings work best for you, I'm free Monday 1/13 or Thursday 1/16 from 8 a.m. to 10:30 a.m. If afternoons are best, I could do Tuesday 1/14 after 3 p.m. or Wednesday 1/15 over the lunch hour (noon). Please let me know if any of those times will work for you! I'm also open to suggestions for great coffee shops or lunch spots near you for your convenience.

I'm looking forward to meeting you!

Sincerely,

Abby

Cold email example (after referral):

Dear Monica,

My name is Abby Bajuniemi, and I'm currently a visiting assistant professor at [college]. I'm currently [transitioning to, researching the field of] UX, and I recently met with Jenny Vang at [company] to learn more about their UX practice. She suggested I get in touch with you. I would love to meet with you at your convenience to learn more about your UX practice and experience at [company].

Sincerely,

Abby

Thank-you example:

Dear María,

I really enjoyed chatting with you today. It was so interesting to hear about [company]'s UX practice and what you do on a day-to-day basis. Hearing your experience really solidified that this is an excellent career fit for me. I'm also really excited about the opportunity to meet

Andrew over at [company]. Thank you so much for offering to introduce us and for your time today.

Sincerely,

Abby

Of course, some interactions weren't fruitful. I talked to someone from a recruiting firm who started out our phone call with, "First, can I just say I am SO IMPRESSED you have a PhD? I think if I had a PhD, I'd wear a cape all the time." What? Okay. They seemed interested in placing me in the field, but then lowballed me ($45,000) because they didn't understand my value. They also did some borderline unethical editing on my résumé. I did not work with that firm. However, the majority were amazing people who wanted to help any way they could.

Back to the job I didn't like. I had a few people in my back pocket who were enthusiastic about helping me find a job. They knew about this first job and that it was a first step, not an ideal position. I reached out to them and said, "So, this new gig isn't quite what I expected, and I'd love to find something that's a better fit for my skills and career direction. Know of anything?" One woman said she did and to let her know if I applied because she knew the hiring manager. The job seemed ideal: I'd be doing UX research at a company rated one of the "best places to work" in my state. I applied and then emailed my friend to let her know. This was a Friday. Monday morning, my friend emailed me with a copy of the (amazing) email she sent the hiring manager on my behalf. Within an hour, the talent acquisition person at the company called to set up an interview.

Nonacademic Interviewing

You would think that nonacademic interviewing would be different from academic interviewing, but the two-part process for my second job was pretty similar to the campus interview for my visiting assistant professorship. The first was a "group interview" for me and three other candidates in which we were given a fictional problem to solve: help a restaurant develop an at-the-table ordering interface.

The UX team was all there, and the candidates were split into pairs for each phase of the interview, which mimicked each phase of this fictional UX project. At the end of the process, we presented our designs to the team and then launched into a Q&A. In total, the interview took about two hours.

I did well in the group interview because of my ability to talk to a crowd and formulate intelligent questions about others' work. As soon as I got home, I sent a thank-you email to the talent acquisition person who had set up my interview, and within an hour of my sending it, he responded by saying the team was "blown away" and that I had "knocked it out of the park." I was invited back to an individual interview.

This interview was committee-style, with about four people from the team plus the manager. It was kind of like a defense, but more friendly. I can't remember many specific questions—I had a lot of adrenaline going—but I can offer some general topics.

They asked me how I got interested in UX and why I was changing careers. I was honest. I said that there was a lack of true career trajectory in academia, and that I was looking for a career that would offer me advancement and ability to carve out a path for myself. They asked me what I liked most about teaching. Since I went to grad school a bit later in life, I had a seemingly strange trajectory from veterinary medicine to graduate school to a visiting assistant professorship to industry. They asked me to talk about that trajectory. They also asked me what part of the advertised job I felt was weakest for me. I was honest there, too, and said that I was pretty weak in the specific tools used in UX work, but that I was confident in my ability to learn them when needed. Within twenty-four hours of that interview, I had a job offer with paid vacation and full benefits. My timeline from the first job to this one wasn't long, but I'd never have this job without my network.

I also want to acknowledge this: it hasn't been easy. I have PTSD and some level of social anxiety. Putting myself out there was hard at first, but it got easier. Particularly if you're introverted, networking is laborious and needs care, just like a pet or a plant. Take it seriously and devote time to cultivating your network. You never know where the next opportunity will come from. It also hasn't been easy adjusting to life outside academia, but that comes with time. I still struggle with impostor syndrome. It is getting a little better as I get more comfortable in my role, but it's still there. Leaving work at work is amazing. Getting paid for what I do is amazing.

My Second Job

My second job title was "UX designer," but, unlike in academia, titles mean little in my field. You can be a UX designer, an interaction designer, a UX researcher, an information architect, a UX professional, and a UX architect, among others, and do the exact things I did daily. You'll hopefully begin to see how my academic background transferred to this job and how you can use some of your skills and talents in industry.

In 2017 I was sent to the Netherlands and Spain to talk to customers about their use of technology. To prepare, I took the business goals and formulated an interview guide to help frame the questions I would ask the interviewees. I interviewed customers in different roles within their companies, in Spanish and English, and watched them use the technology they have currently as they did their jobs. I showed them new technology in development and asked them to use it and give me feedback on the functionality that exists and what is missing that they would need to do their jobs. Just in that one trip, I used my language skills, research and research design skills, and presentation skills.

I also collaborated with other members of my team when designing technology solutions. That often involved hashing out a user's workflow, figuring out different elements of the interface, helping mock up prototypes in different design software, and giving feedback on designs that had already been created.[4]

Surprisingly, I've gotten to develop workshops that draw upon my linguistics background. The first, titled "Language and Gender in the Workplace," was presented to our Women in Tech group and got a great reception. I taught attendees about language ideology and gendered language, and how women can support themselves and one another in the workplace when confronted with blatant or covert sexism using language and actions.

The second drew upon concepts from semantics and phonology to talk about "mental models" in UX, which describe how the brain organizes information and knows (or doesn't know) how to use an interface. I presented this workshop to my internal team and was then invited (by a networking contact) to give this workshop to a cohort of UX students at a local boot camp. That was well-received, and I was immediately invited back to the boot camp to give the lesson to the next cohort! Because of my experience in teaching as well as survey and assessment design, I was also brought into the training group at my job to help them deliver workshops to the company as well as redesign some of their materials.

Finally, my specific linguistics knowledge is interesting to people in the field of UX as well as content strategy (closely related to UX), and I've been invited to speak at the local UXPA chapter about how language presents usability and accessibility issues, and I've had this same talk accepted at a local tech conference. My industry life doesn't look that dissimilar from my

4. I am learning software on the fly, and thankfully, most of it is way more user-friendly than, say, Blackboard.

academic life, to be honest. It just pays (way) more, I have the potential to grow exponentially, and people are excited about my experience and supportive of me.

Are there negatives? Sure. Office politics still happen, and there will still always be people who are intimidated by your PhD. Who cares? You're getting paid to do cool shit, and unlike in academia, you can find another job in your area if you don't like what you're doing. Also unlike in academia, "you never know" actually holds true; you never know who might think of you when an opportunity arises. You never know how your PhD topic and skills will be used outside academia. There are so many ways to use your skills and knowledge and so many directions you can go.

11

How I Left My PhD in English Behind and Learned to Love the Stacks

BRIAN FLOTA

Ten years ago, when I started as a new visiting assistant professor in an English Department at a public university in the Midwest, I had no idea I'd wind up being one of two humanities librarians at James Madison University (JMU). And my life is all the better for it.

Way back then, in August 2007, I moved around 1,300 miles to begin my new academic life. I had obtained my PhD in English a year earlier, and I was convinced that my new position would instantly parlay itself into a tenure-track job. (Spoiler: It didn't work out that way.) The training I received in my PhD program came nowhere close to preparing me for the academic job market. Furthermore, it did little to suggest an alternate career path for me or my colleagues besides a tenure-track position in an English Department.

Ultimately, I became disillusioned by the profession I had devoted so much of my adult life to. By my fourth full year as a visiting assistant professor at the same university—with that elusive tenure-track job still beyond my grasp—I decided to leave the profession. If you already have your PhD in a humanities discipline but are having no luck on the job market, I'll provide a blueprint for moving in a new direction and making the best of the expertise gained during your PhD experience.

I'll discuss why I made the decision to leave and, after some intense self-analysis and a leap of vocational faith, pursue a new career path in librarianship. Apropos of this discussion, I will look back at what I could have done differently while I was pursuing my PhD and a career as an English professor. I want to inform current PhDs about the things that can derail their career aspirations.

Pre-Doctorization: Being a First-Generation College Student

I am a first-generation college student. Growing up, my mother told me again and again I was going to college. Eventually it became something I took for granted and never thought about much. When I started college in 1994, as a commuting student (I lived at home for my undergraduate years), I was anxious. Much to my surprise, it took only a few weeks for me to realize that I loved college and that academia was the place for me. Being a first-generation student didn't present me with too many obstacles at the time.

One thing I was not prepared for, though, was graduate school. In my junior year, I had it in my mind to pursue a PhD in English. I got some advice from faculty members who were generally encouraging, with only a few issuing words of caution. My family did not fully understand the point of graduate schools generally, so they were far more cautious. Not knowing the application due date cycle, I ultimately had to put off my decision for a year because I missed most of the deadlines.

After graduating from college, I made my big push, applying to twelve schools. I got accepted into four. One program—a private, non–Ivy League university—offered me acceptance into their straight PhD track with a partial scholarship. So that is where I went to get my degree. Though funding is clearly an issue for many pursuing a graduate degree, choosing a program solely based on the package they offer you is probably not the wisest decision. If you are a first-generation student and are thinking about going to graduate school, make sure you reach out to as many people with graduate school experience as possible and *take their advice*. Some colleges have staff members who are trained to provide guidance for first-generation students. Seek those people out. Also, look up nonprofit organizations geared toward first-generation students (such as I'm First) that can provide additional resources.

Doctorization: The Doctoring

In the summer of 1999, I made my 2,700-mile trek from California to the East Coast to begin earning my PhD in English. At the time I was a twenty-three-year-old dreamer who thought the program would inform my own creative writing. I had given few considerations beyond that to my future professional prospects. I was going to read lots of great books! Because neither of my parents attended graduate school, nor did any of my friends, I had little idea what I was doing beyond my schoolwork.

That first year, our program had a boilerplate "Introduction to Graduate

Studies" course. With the exception of one class that focused on recent graduates who went into professions outside academia, there was little attention given to alternate career paths. The class did a lousy job of introducing us to the profession, though we did have a mock-conference to get a sense of what that experience is like. Essentially, it was geared toward scaring students lacking the mental fortitude to finish the program, so that they would leave before they invested too much of themselves into it.

Here's what the class should have done—cover the spectrum of possible transferable skills a PhD in English could give a prospective student, such as the following:

- developing keen analytical skills
- gaining management experience through teaching a class
- completing a long-standing project (for instance, a thesis or dissertation)
- public speaking (through talks or conferencing)
- editing
- making connections between technology, teaching, and research.

These are just a few things we could have learned, which would have been immeasurably valuable. Unfortunately, the class perpetuated the unspoken perception that the only acceptable career path for a PhD in English is a tenure-track job in the discipline and that anything else is a failure.

When we did the mock-conference, we discovered there was no departmental policy or guidelines regarding conference papers. For instance, should we try to have papers accepted at two or more conferences a year? Similarly, there was not a policy for how we should treat the twenty- to forty-page papers we would produce in our graduate seminars. Should we treat them like publishable, submittable scholarly essays? Or should we treat them as papers that we turn in at the end of the semester? Since there was no philosophy regarding our seminar papers, the answer to the first question was "I dunno" and, implicitly, "Yes" to the second.

As a result of the lack of institutional and programmatic guidance provided by the Introduction to Graduate Studies class, I developed lazy professional habits. I occasionally participated in conferences, but not as much as I should have. I put little effort into networking. I was not active in professional organizations, especially those with graduate student branches. Worst of all, our program did little to encourage us to think about any alternative means of employment beyond adjuncting.

When it was time for me to start seriously considering the job market in

2004, I found the advice I received from the graduate faculty to be largely ineffective. The faculty (as at most universities) seemed to think the job market would be a breeze for my cohort. This stems from multiple factors. First, most of the graduate faculty, unlike me, had Ivy League degrees. Second, they had jobs. If it wasn't that difficult for them to get jobs, then there's no way it would be that difficult for me, or so goes this line of thinking. Third, when they got their tenure-track jobs, most of them prior to the late 1990s, the market was less competitive and much easier to navigate. Fourth, and perhaps most injuriously, there was a profound lack of awareness of or sensitivity to the glut of English PhDs on the market.

My program did not have a plan for teaching those who did want to pursue the tenure track how to successfully compose a cover letter, write an effective curriculum vitae, or to conduct an in-person, phone, or webcam interview. Nor did it have a plan for those who wanted to move on from the discipline.

Adjunctification; or, the Trap

As part of my graduate assistantship, I taught Freshman Composition classes as well as a few American and African American literature survey courses. With an established track record for quality teaching, I soon became an adjunct in a new program on campus: University Writing. Several of the full-time faculty had previously been adjuncts at the university. Given this continuity, the faculty would vaguely promise that such jobs were available now that I was all-but-dissertation (ABD). These kinds of half-hearted promises are used to manipulate adjuncts into staying loyal to a particular institution to exploit their labor.

I ended up adjuncting for two years. None of my similarly situated colleagues attained tenure-track jobs during my time there. At least my home department, English, was explicit that they would not hire their own PhDs into tenure-track positions (to ensure workplace and intellectual diversity, or so they claimed). During this period, I ended up adjuncting at one other local public university and at a local community college.

In my third year on the job market—with nothing to show for it—I scored a visiting assistant professor position in the Midwest. It was a one-year contract, renewable for up to three years. It offered benefits and a higher salary, which were welcomed. I was not required to have any service commitments, which proved to be a double-edged sword.

Although this arrangement limited my service experience, it gave me more free time to work on my scholarship. Yes, I had been exposed to internal discord at my previous institution, but I was not prepared for the factions and internecine battles in my new department. For instance, the tenured and tenure-track faculty rarely (if ever) consorted with the visiting assistant professors, whom they dubbed "VAPs" (which was an insulting nickname meant to echo "vapid"). This severely limited my opportunities to seek out mentors. There were no people in the department who shared my scholarly interests, which made it difficult to receive useful feedback on my scholarship.

Now half a country removed from my mentors on the East Coast, I was left to my own devices. I made short-sighted, impulsive decisions ("publish or perish") regarding where to submit my scholarship. This ultimately harmed my career prospects. Nobody told me how to deal with strongly worded, mean-spirited feedback from peer reviewers or how to handle rejection. I was productive in terms of scholarship: I published a book, two encyclopedia entries, an essay in a peer-reviewed online journal, and another in an essay collection. But none of these pieces appeared in prestigious venues. I doggedly adhered to the path of least resistance. Rudderless in both my profession and in my own department, I became friends mostly with graduate students. This professional isolation, combined with the nagging suspicion that I was serving as an ineffective mentor to new friends, withered my confidence and interest in my areas of specialization.

Compounding these problems was the Great Recession, which reared its ugly head as I began the second year of my VAP position. That year, I applied for thirty-eight jobs, ten of which were canceled. By the time I finished my fourth year in the position, I had applied for 250 jobs since I entered the market in 2005. I netted a total of ten phone interviews, four of which happened that first year (when I was ABD), and zero campus visits. That means that I was getting one interview for every twenty-five applications submitted. Meanwhile, two of my colleagues, who unlike me had tenure-track positions, soon took jobs at better schools despite having no publications. Both of them, of course, had Ivy League degrees. I was now five years out from receiving my PhD. Conventional wisdom within the discipline suggests that from that point forward, the chances of landing a tenure-track position are basically nil.

How I Learned from My Mistakes and Came to Love Networking

In my third year as a visiting assistant professor, I entertained the idea of going to library school. I thought hard about librarianship because of my previous experience working in libraries. My first job was as an undergraduate working in the main library. There, I worked on a project to transfer the contents of the card catalog into online catalog records. During this experience, I taught myself the basics of cataloging and the Library of Congress classification system. This was work I really enjoyed doing because it appealed to the list maker in me.

After graduation, I got my first full-time job working as a library assistant at a small private university in Southern California. There I did much of the same work, but I had increased responsibilities, including importing catalog records from the Online Computer Library Center, or OCLC (the company that runs the world's largest union catalog—or catalog of catalogs), processing books (by adding barcodes, due date slips, and magnetic theft-prevention strips), and managing three undergraduate students.

I enjoyed spending time with my colleagues as much as I enjoyed the work. I found librarians to be smart, personable, quirky, and encouraging. Years later, after I had completed my PhD in English, these same qualities made me wonder why I hadn't pursued a career in librarianship earlier. Furthermore, I found a disappointingly high percentage of the people associated with English Departments to be aloof, discouraging, deceptively competitive, and beholden to structural systems of power they claimed to be undermining in their own scholarship. After thinking long and hard about this, I decided to apply to a library school graduate program.

Not wishing to repeat my PhD experience—where I was in a middle-of-the-road program that cheapened my job market currency—I applied to one library program, a highly ranked one. I reached out to the dean of the graduate school, explaining my situation and background. He responded promptly and told me to apply. It was encouraging that he was also an English PhD who had changed careers. I applied and was accepted. I deferred for a year because I thought the forthcoming coedited essay collection I was working on might help my tenure-track English lit job prospects.

It did not. I received one job interview but did not get a campus visit. Now I was finished pursuing a career as an English professor. So I made a risky decision: I left a job with benefits for massive college loan debt and the life of a graduate student (in my mid-thirties). Trapped in a dead-end academic job, stuck grading never-ending stacks of uninspired papers, and losing my desire to teach (I went from making new syllabi every semester to re-teaching the same material because it was less hassle), I felt like it was the only option remaining to salvage my career and to get value out of my PhD. Now it was time to get an MS in library and information science and get started on a new career. I was newly inspired by the possibilities awaiting me. I was also racked with anxiety about potential unemployment, debt, and failure.

Just Like Starting Over

I arrived in Illinois two months before the start of my first semester to get some volunteer experience (since it had been over a decade since I had worked in a library) and to conduct some informational interviews. An informational interview consists of identifying people in a field of interest and asking them a series of questions about professional training, breaking into the field, career trajectory, finding mentors, skills and experience required, and workflow. Soon I started volunteering at the public library near where I lived. Then I set up meetings with six librarians and library school faculty that were associated with my areas of interest (special collections, literature) or had some clout in the department (the dean, the director of library units). Despite having a PhD in a field without a ton of them, I knew I still had to compete on the job market with younger, more energetic, and tech-savvier students. So it was time to catch up—quickly.

Once classes started, I was determined to get good grades but put more energy into networking, something I barely did while pursuing my PhD. I joined student groups for professional organizations, such as the American Library Association (ALA) and the Special Libraries Association (SLA), both of which offer discount rates for graduate students. At some of the events hosted by these groups, librarians from the region would come and speak about their work and the skills and experience it required. At one, I met staff from a local special library (a special library is one that is not a public or school library) and subsequently contacted them to see if they currently had any volunteering opportunities available. They did.

After a few months with them, I was offered a ten-hour-a-week job that would parlay itself into a graduate assistantship the following academic year. Because of my networking efforts, I landed valuable library experience at a place where I had to do a little bit of everything (circulation desk duties, collection development, event planning, and database development).

Instead of developing a specialization, I decided to take classes from a wide array of subjects within the library and information science discipline. I emphasized the essentials: reference, cataloging, and metadata; library management; archives; special collections; and displays. I figured this could give me some wiggle room on the job market. One of the drawbacks of a PhD is overspecialization, especially if it is in an area that is oversaturated or less in demand, like mine (twentieth-century American literature). Based on the library job advertisements I was looking at, general skills were just as in demand as specialized ones because of the evolving needs of each specific library and their users.

Here's some advice based on what I've learned so far (see the next section for more). Always look at job ads in the profession you are choosing to join. They can be insightful and help you become aware of emerging trends in the field.

At the same time, address potential weaknesses in your coursework. During my time as a PhD student and adjunct, my computing skills stalled just as the technology grew. Because of this deficiency, I took several classes. I learned various metadata schema, became more familiar with HTML and XML, and took a class on databases, which, I kid you not, was the most difficult class I ever took in my twenty-five years of schooling. Though I would still not claim to be especially strong in these areas, I became more conversant regarding user experience, responsive design, digital humanities, and open access efforts.

Knowing your strengths when choosing areas of interest can steer you in the right direction and help you avoid potential rabbit holes. Since I had worked for a dozen years in academia, academic librarianship was well suited to my experience. Though my dream job in library school was to be a special collections librarian, that track is fraught with many of the same perils as tenure-track teaching positions are—way too many qualified people (many with PhDs, in fact) for too few positions.

Despite this, I still put in hours of volunteer time with the special collections unit at the university, working on collection development projects. Even though I did not get a job in a special collections library or unit, the experience with collection development was directly applicable to many of the academic librarian job ads I was seeing.

I also learned from past mistakes that networking is invaluable. As an introvert, I don't naturally enjoy networking. But since I wanted to get the most out of my degree, I made sure to engage in as many networking opportunities as possible. Earlier, I mentioned conducting informational interviews with librarians and librarian faculty. One of those informational interviews paid off. Nearly a year after I talked to the literature librarian at my school, she remembered our conversation and offered me a second graduate assistantship at the university's literature library, so I could connect my expertise in literature with my continued development in library school. That was huge because that specific experience translated into the job I have now.

Though they can be expensive, especially for cash-strapped graduate students, I also encourage you to attend professional conferences. They offer great networking experiences and can expose you to a multitude of potential employers. While pursuing my PhD in English, I did attend some conferences, but I tended to present the occasional paper and didn't really take advantage of the networking opportunities. In library school, I drastically changed that mind-set. I attended some major library conferences, such as the Special Libraries Association (SLA) and the Association of College and Research Libraries (ACRL) conferences, and shared my business cards with as many people as possible. At the SLA conference, I attended a useful workshop to help job applicants boost the quality of their résumé or CV. The next year, I attended the conference again and won a stipend (with most of the expenses paid).

Nothing in the Way

In my five years on the job market as ABD or with a PhD in English, I applied to roughly 250 tenure-track jobs, received ten job interviews, and got zero campus visits. Four of those interviews came when I was ABD. In my first three months on the job market while in my final semester of the MS in library and information science program, I applied to fifty jobs. I got seven interviews and two campus visits.

During the interview process, make sure you know the basic rules of your chosen profession as they relate to interviewing. I bombed my first interview because of one simple reason—the first question. During interviews for tenure-track jobs in English, the first question usually focuses on one's current big research project. For ABDs, this is the dissertation. For those with the PhD, it is often a book project. However, unbeknownst to me at the time, library job interviews tend to start with some variation of the following question: What compelled you to apply for this position? Or, Why do you feel this job would be a good fit for you? Because I was unprepared for this relatively simple question in my first phone interview, I floundered the rest of the way. In subsequent interviews, I had much better answers to this initial question, and that made answering every other question much easier.

Know your competition. When I went on the job market, my "competition" was often people twelve to fourteen years younger, since I started library school later. Having a PhD has some advantages, but it by no means makes you a "slam dunk" on the job market. A PhD (and other potential work history) can make potential employers presume you'll be wanting a higher salary, which may price you out of certain entry-level positions. Younger applicants will likely be cheaper to hire. As with ABDs, younger applicants are often perceived to have more potential than those with more experience.

When applying for various jobs, demonstrate your *transferable skills* from your experiences as a graduate student and adjunct:

1. Management experience: managing a classroom, shepherding a large research project such as a dissertation or a monograph.
2. Project management, specifically: I coedited a book, which involved fourteen different writers and a publisher, which illustrated that I could handle big projects.
3. Organizational skills: human resources experience, advising, and committee work.
4. Subject expertise: you might not currently have expertise in a new field, but you can show how you gained expertise in other areas.
5. Writing and editing skills.
6. Critical analysis.
7. The spirit of innovation and intervention: as a scholar you discovered a new subject worthy of study, or you changed the existing conversation about it.
8. Collaboration with students and faculty, if you decide to stay in academia or in education.
9. Public speaking skills: leading a class, presenting at conferences or university events.
10. Computing expertise: web design, content management systems like Blackboard or Canvas, coding, social media.

These are just a few of the broad ways in which your previous, but seemingly unrelated, experience can help ease you into a new profession. Now, when I am on search committees, I often ask applicants about how their previous non-library experiences inform their approach to the profession.

Occasionally a job ad will come along that is perfectly suited to your experience. And, better yet, if your networking efforts connect you in some way to that position, your preparation will have been put to good use. While I was on the job market for a library position, few were tailored specifically toward "literature" or "English" librarians. Therefore, when those positions came up, I applied for them.

After I applied for the position of English librarian (as it was then called) at James Madison University, I mentioned it to my graduate supervisor at the literature library. She happened to know the librarian who had previously held the position and set up an informational interview with her. After our talk, I went into the phone interview with confidence, not cockiness. I formed a great rapport with the search committee and ended the call feeling good about my prospects. Going into the campus visit, which I had never done before, I was nervous because I had not spoken in front of a large group since I left my visiting assistant professor gig two years earlier. I was also worried about my lack of library instruction and general lack of librarian experience. So I put together a presentation that combined my English literature background, my previous teaching experience, and my vision of librarianship. And it was a success!

What I'm Doing Now

I am currently a library liaison to James Madison University's English, Theatre and Dance, and Foreign Languages, Literatures, and Cultures Departments. I am responsible for collection development in those areas (the purchasing of monographs and the management of journal and database subscriptions). I work with faculty in those departments to order materials that are foundational to those disciplines and that support their curricula. I am also responsible for teaching what are called one-shot instruction sessions. In these sessions, I speak to a class of undergraduate (and occasionally graduate) students for one or two class periods about information literacy as it relates to the course they are taking. That can include teaching them how to access and navigate general or subject-specific databases, conduct productive searches, find relevant print resources, find credible pieces of scholarship, differentiate between primary and secondary sources, use interlibrary loan, or ask better research questions. Another major component of my work is reference consultation. If students or faculty are having difficulty navigating any of these processes and need assistance, I am available to assist them.

Many of the duties of my job are directly transferable from my PhD experience: teaching, subject expertise, research. Furthermore, this is a tenure-track position. This means that in addition to the duties listed above, I am also required to produce scholarship (the focus of a PhD program) and provide service—through committee work—to the library, to JMU, or to the profession.

There are many aspects of my previous experience which have come in handy in my current position. As liaison with the English Department, I have formed numerous productive relationships with faculty members. With one colleague I collaborated to put on the First Annual Pulp Studies Symposium, which highlighted our collection of pulp magazines from the 1920s to the 1950s and brought together scholars from across the United States. Another colleague and I were awarded a grant to provide funding to develop a collection of African American comic books and graphic novels. I also presented a paper at a JMU conference devoted to African American poetry (put together by an English Department faculty member) on the work of Ishmael Reed, who was the author I concentrated on the most in my previous career.

I have been at JMU now for four years. I love my job. While it is sometimes easy to look back on my previous experience as one of failure, ultimately it was not. Sure, I had to take a windy and often rocky path to get where I am today. But without my PhD and experience as an adjunct, as discouraging as it was at times, I would not be prepared for the job I have today. My passion for research, collections and collection development, and teaching, as it turns out, are better used in the library than in the literature classroom.

Plus librarians are *still* the greatest group of coworkers I've ever had. It is easy to be disappointed in yourself for not "making it" in the field in which you obtained your PhD because of the financial, temporal, intellectual, and mental costs accumulated for your efforts. But if there is one thing to learn from my experience, it is that it is possible to transform that disappointment into a new, and ultimately more fulfilling, career.

12

Education, Writing, Entrepreneurship

Creating Impact through Communities

RUSUL ALRUBAIL

The summer of 2015, I received a phone call that would forever alter my career. "Rusul, I am afraid I have some bad news," the chair of my department said. "Starting next winter, there will no longer be contract faculty positions at the college." My heart dropped; my mind raced. What did that mean? Would I still have a job? How would this affect me? Of course, it did. I wasn't tenured yet, and it would impact me tremendously.

I didn't know what to think. "Why?" was my first question. The answer I received didn't make sense to me, something about unionized faculty and how the college couldn't support unionized staff anymore.

I had never thought about what I would do if I wasn't teaching. I spent long nights practicing for a scheduled interview for a tenure-track position in the hopes of becoming a tenured faculty member at the college. After not landing the tenure position the first round, I went through two more interviews during my last year at the college. And with each interview, I received some feedback and decided to work harder next time around in the hope that I would finally have a secure tenure-track position at the college, which I loved so dearly. Some of the interview feedback I received was that when I did the teaching demo, I spent quite a bit of time mapping out ideas on the board with my back turned to the interviewers. I needed to face them and make more eye contact. Ironically, these demos were for courses I was already teaching: College English and composition or literature optional courses.

I loved working with my students. And when anyone asks me what I miss the most after leaving academia, I tell them: the students.

When I explored the teaching options available at my college, I found out that they were unfeasible for me as a new mom of two girls and as an English instructor. I was given two options: I could either work fewer than six classroom hours or more than fifteen hours. One wouldn't cover the bills, let alone child care. The other would be doing a disservice to my students. My essay grading would go through the roof, which would mean that I would barely have time to give my students feedback on their writing. Instead, I would be simply marking papers and giving out grades. These options also didn't make sense for many of the seasoned contract faculty members, especially the senior faculty, who relied on health insurance through their union contracts.

The college decided to stop hiring contract faculty, which meant that there was no longer a union to stand behind part-time faculty. Without a union, health benefits for instructors also disappeared.

I decided to leave because I got into teaching to begin with to help students, not to be disempowered as a faculty member. I wanted to help students see that their voice mattered. That their writing was important and could make a difference. More importantly, I wanted to help students learn to actually like writing. It sounds like a simple task, but it wasn't. One of the hardest parts of teaching at the college, especially an applied technology college, was to get students to see how writing was relevant to them inside and outside their industries. The most rewarding feeling was having a student say, "I actually enjoy writing now."

I left the classroom. And even though I did, I knew that I still wanted to help students and support teachers in one way or another. I just had to figure what that would look like. The transition from the classroom was one of the toughest things I've ever had to encounter in my adult life. It wasn't easy for me to figure out the next steps in my career or what it meant that I wasn't teaching. Needless to say, there was a lot of emotional turmoil and sleepless nights, but also I felt like a failure. I had failed to land a tenure position, and as a result, I had failed to secure my dream career.

Little did I know that there was a whole world out there for me that I still have yet to tap into fully. It's been three years since I left the classroom, and I did not experience the amount of professional and personal growth there that I am experiencing right now.

Out of the Classroom

I had a baby and a toddler when I left the classroom. A part of me thought I should focus on them. Being a new mom, especially a working mom in academia, I began to hear that mothers should focus on their kids at this stage in life and that they'll always have a choice to return to teaching. I disagree with this sentiment completely, but at that time, I was still struggling to figure out what to do. I began to see how hard it was to be a mother and teach at the same time at the college. The system was deliberately pushing me out. What was I supposed to believe other than that perhaps I didn't belong there?

As a result, I took a break for a few months to figure out the next steps in my career. What should I be doing? Should I apply for a job? Go back to school and maybe finally get my PhD?

One day, I decided to join Twitter after following a motherhood conference that used a hashtag. Little did I know that the world of education and learning communities was simply 140 characters away. When I joined Twitter, I was able to connect with educators from all over the world and discuss educational issues.

Most of these connections came about through Twitter chats, and slowly I began to see that blogging is also a component that connected educators can leverage to expand their 140-character conversations. It's not enough to simply answer questions and have conversations on Twitter chats; I needed to also reflect on and respond to the topics by blogging and sharing the blog post with other educators to expand the conversation.

Writing

When I started blogging and publishing my work, it was the first time I had published work outside an academic setting. At first, I was uncomfortable. To be writing and publishing work on websites and blogs outside academia seemed to me something that would damage my credibility as a writer. In academia, there is a culture of publishing credibility, which means we publish our writing in a reputable journal. The moment we enter graduate school, we begin to see how our reputations as writers always rely on where we publish our work. Publishing in online publications was frowned upon by colleagues and peers.

And yet, something drove me to keep writing and publishing. More importantly, something drove me to keep sharing my writing with my network of people to whom I grew close professionally. When I connected with other educators, they became my support network to get my work out there. Many of them encouraged me to continue to share my voice and my stories, and that helped me to keep going. I felt like my voice, as cliché as it sounds, truly does matter and that some people will benefit from reading my articles.

At first, I started writing on Medium. I was encouraged to write there by my partner, who gave me solid advice: write on Medium and see how often you'll write. If you're consistent, create a website of your own. And that's what I did.

My first couple of blog posts discussed my experience at the college and some thoughts on professional development. Then my posts shifted to share some of my best practices in the classroom. I wrote about some of my favorite instructional strategies when it comes to writing, and student engagement at the college level.

Becoming a Writer

The most important aspect of becoming a writer is to write for yourself. I started out writing because I had a lot to say about my experiences in the education system. I didn't know if I would get readership, and that wasn't my goal.

Of course, once I got readership, engagement, and traction, I started to consider writing about topics that would resonate with my audience. This is where writers sometimes go down a rabbit hole. When writers focus only on writing pieces that resonate with their audience, there is a chance that they will miss out on writing things they truly care about and topics that come from the heart, thus losing authenticity.

While I wrote pieces about teaching, learning, and education, I was not writing about things I truly cared about within those sectors. I wanted to write about race, equity, and social justice in teaching and learning. I didn't feel comfortable doing that because I feared that I did not have the audience.

I set up my own Wordpress site, used a free theme, and wrote about things that mattered, but I continued to feel disconnected from my own work. I thought to myself, maybe I need to find different outlets that would help me attract a new, even larger audience. I thought that would help me to connect to my own writing.

I have to admit that when I reached out to education publications I avoided pitching to academic journals focused on higher education. I knew that academic journals are gatekeepers. They do not accept work easily and ask to make significant changes to your story and voice. And at that time, writing while being a stay-at-home mom was not an easy task. The time I had was precious, and I didn't want to waste my time and energy on publishers who did not appreciate my writing style.

The first publication I reached out to was *Edutopia*, an education resource website run by the George Lucas Foundation. Later I also wrote for the *Guardian*, *PBS NewsHour*, the ASCD's *Educational Leadership* publication, and the International Literacy Association, among others. I'd like to share the most effective way that I found to pitch an idea to editors.

My Strategy on Writing a Strong Pitch

In and of itself, writing a pitch is a craft. I am still learning this as we speak, because for each editor I meet and each publication I work with, the conversation and the work process often differs. Each publication will have a different set of standards and guidelines for pitches. It's best to check their website, usually under the "Contact Us," "About Us," or "Contribute" sections to see if they have provided these guidelines.

Here are several tips to use when writing a pitch to editors and publishers:

- Topics for the pitch must be relevant and current according to daily events and the news cycles. If you're sending a pitch to an education publication, then it needs to be relevant to their calendar and/or current topics in education.
- A pitch should be no more than two to three paragraphs in length, especially for a 600–700 word piece. Keep it short and concise. Focus on why it is important to write this piece now.
- Include a description of the argument you're making and the sources you plan on using. If possible, link to the sources or write out their names, so that the editor will see how these sources relate to the story.
- Next, make sure to write a bit about yourself. Why are you the right person to write this story? Provide a link to your website or portfolio of past writings.

Some Realities for New Writers

If you're a new writer, you most likely won't have a writing portfolio. Here is where your blog posts can help as examples. If you're a recent graduate, make sure to upload your work digitally (if it does not violate any copyright rules, of course) in order for it to be easily shareable and accessible to editors.

Many writing platforms and publications require you to have social media accounts so that they can share your work via those accounts. This helps your writing reach a wider audience and helps your readers to connect with you. Set up Twitter and Facebook accounts, if you don't have them, just for publishing purposes and to share your work on those platforms.

And, of course, when sharing your work it's important to also leverage your connections! If you're already on social media, try to connect with editors on Twitter and ask them if they're accepting pitches. Often if they are, they say so in their bios. But sometimes they're open to hearing from you to see if your pitch will work for their publication.

Writer's Compensation

Many new writers shy away from asking for compensation or even checking to see if the publisher pays contributing authors. Depending on your priorities, there are different ways to handle this issue. When I first started out, I needed to write and get published in different educational outlets that were prominent and were aligned with my mission and purpose. I didn't worry too much about getting paid as a writer; my priority was to build up my reputation as a credible writer.

Now, for a Muslim woman of color, developing credibility can be a bit problematic. The voices of people like me, and other women of color, are not the norm. And as a result, we bring perspectives, knowledge, and points of view that are fresh and often help to shift the cultural landscape of the publication. It's important to recognize that all writers need to be compensated for their work. It's also crucial to realize that women of color often are underappreciated and underpaid for writing and sharing their knowledge, even though their knowledge and the perspectives they provide benefit the publication in terms of both traffic and audience engagement.

To learn more about these processes myself, I reached out to friends who were established writers already and asked them how they navigate the writing scene. I recognized that it was a lot of work for them to figure all of this out on their own, and I really appreciated the knowledge they shared with me. Many people aren't always willing to help for many reasons, including the ones I mentioned above. It's really hard to navigate the system and processes, and sharing knowledge, especially for free, should not be one of our expectations.

While getting paid for my writing wasn't a priority in my early writing career, it started to become a symbol of appreciation for my work. Now, I don't shy away from asking editors if there is a budget for a piece that I pitched. And often, they tell me this information when they reply. Then it's up to me to decide if that compensation works well with my priorities, time, effort, and getting published with that specific publication.

Building Your Professional Learning Network

A semester before leaving the college, I created my first social media account on Twitter. Before that, we were warned to not have any social media presence as educators. That was one of the things that I regret not doing, because it hindered me from having access to opportunities for my professional and personal development throughout my teaching career.

Social media gave me access to a wealth of knowledge and resources from global connections. It also allowed me to grow and develop personally and professionally while helping me to build and sustain communities around my own learning. I used Twitter as a tool to connect with people all over the world. And more importantly, I also used Twitter as a tool to grow my own network of connections. I've outlined my strategies below.

- *Engage*: When you're on social media for professional and even personal development, it's important to engage with people whose work you admire or who are discussing issues and topics that are important to you. It's totally okay for new users to lurk at first before diving into the waters of chats, news, and discussion threads. However, in order to get the most out of social media as a professional learning network, you need to engage with others. Engagement with others shows others that you're an authentic individual who's connecting to learn and grow, and that often leads to greater impact professionally and personally.
- *Share*: Be sure to show your authenticity and originality by sharing your own work and resources that you find interesting and useful for others. Many people connect with people who are sharing work that aligns with their values, interests, and beliefs, and many people will happen upon the work you share and connect with you, which would give you the opportunity to expand your network and connect with like-minded individuals.
- *Amplify*: It's often not enough for you to simply engage and share; you also need to amplify others' work. When you do so, it allows you to form a connection and, more importantly, build a strong relationship with them. Also remember that on social media amplifying marginalized voices, which are often unheard and

underrepresented, should be one of your core missions because of the great social impact for those you amplify and their causes.

Becoming an Entrepreneur

After I started writing, many speaking opportunities opened up for me. I started presenting and speaking to educators about race and equity in education. However, these writing and speaking gigs were freelance opportunities and were simply not enough to live on with two kids. As a result, I decided to expand on a project that I had developed with my partner.

When I was teaching, I noticed that there was a gap between what we're telling students regarding writing and what they're actually doing as writers. Some students were able to meet the standard requirements of writing a paragraph or an essay, but were not able to think critically about the topic. And some students were able to think critically, yet grasping writing structure was a difficult task for them.

As a result, my husband, who is the founder of a user experience and design agency, and I decided to create a step-by-step approach to writing. We thought giving students a guided, step-by-step, inquiry-based process would make it easier for them to write an essay or report than asking them to start from scratch.

The step-by-step process was composed of several questions to students about their work, and their answers would form a complete paragraph and/or essay. With permission from my department, we piloted the workbook, which we called *The Writing Project*, in my classes.

The results were fascinating. Students were able to move on from description to analysis. They were able to relate the issues they were discussing to real life, and more importantly, provide their own opinions about the topics. It was a major milestone for me, because I saw how my students struggle and now I see the work they're able to produce with some guided instructions. This system transformed my English-language learners from students who believed that no matter how hard they tried, what they wrote didn't matter, into empowered students who believe that they have opinions and perspectives that others want to hear.

The success of the workbook led us to design an app to help students become better writers. And this app now is a publishing platform for students that contains the same original inquiry-based approach that we laid out in the workbook to help students walk through the process of paragraph and report/essay writing. We created a product that helps students write better and get published. I never call myself this, but I became an entrepreneur the moment we conceived the workbook.

Lessons from the School of Hard Knocks

I entered into the world of entrepreneurship accidentally, but found that this is now the next step in my career. While working on *The Writing Project*, I slowly started to navigate the educational technology industry. I started learning about business development, communications, campaigns, and grants and funding, and for the last couple of months we started to pitch investors to raise a seed round. Many of these conversations did not go so well; apparently I was talking to investors in the same way I talk to educators. That didn't work. I learned to be more firm and confident—something I'm still working on.

It is not an easy landscape to navigate as an educator or as a woman, let alone as a visible Muslim woman. And yet, I am choosing to persevere despite all the obstacles and hurdles in my way.

I am learning constantly, and I have several tips for educators entering the space of entrepreneurship:

- *Don't underestimate your knowledge.* It's easy for educators to believe that our knowledge is limited. We're constantly told that "this is your area" and "this is not your area" of interest. Don't believe that. You know more than you think and if you underestimate your knowledge and experience, then you miss out on many opportunities, and the industry will take advantage of you. Believe in yourself and be willing to do your own research without asking for help. When someone is explaining a concept to you that you already understand, don't be afraid to tell them that you already know this and move the conversation forward.
- *Understand context before everything.* This is, like the first item in this list, not easy for me to apply in my day-to-day interactions, but I am learning that when I engage with potential clients, investors, and customers, it's important to be able to get the full context of where they're coming from before giving away all your thoughts and ideas. Many of those stakeholders are not focusing on the same context you're focusing on, or there might be an underlying assumption that needs to be addressed before diving into the specifics. Therefore, it's important to not shy away from asking questions. It sounds so

simple, and it is something I always advised my students to do, yet it is very difficult to apply. Don't hesitate to steer the conversation the way you'd like it to go to achieve your goals.

- *Don't waste your time!* We hear this often, but as an entrepreneur, I am finding out more and more that I need to organize, plan, and focus better. We can waste so much time doing research, talking to the wrong people, and not prioritizing our tasks. If you'd like to start your own business, it's so important to make effective use of your time and especially to prioritize your tasks. We can get caught up doing things that are not immediately deserving of our attention and miss out on deadlines and opportunities that actually help to pay our bills.

As an educator, a writer, an entrepreneur, and a mom of two kids, I am still learning a lot as I go through all these new life stages and changes. I learned that it's okay to do things you didn't plan on doing. I am also learning to seize opportunities that come my way, and to not let things slip by without at least trying. I am also slowly learning to accept my failures and live with them as part of my growth. That is probably the toughest learning curve for me. It's very hard to recognize your mistakes and failures and just sit with them. And I am learning to do that, while still practicing self-care and not letting it impact my emotional spirit and self-esteem.

Following one's passion is a privilege that not many of us have. If you do have the opportunity to start anew, make sure to do something that you're passionate about. It would be a bonus to do something that you feel strongly will have a positive impact on yourself and others. It's important that you also ask for help and seek support when it comes to career decision-making. Some people will be unhelpful, but many will walk with you, support you, and be there for you when you need anything. Know that you will get through the hard stage very quickly and that you'll learn a lot from your mistakes and failures. Be sure to see your failures as opportunities to learn and grow, so that next time you're prepared and equipped with the necessary tools and experiences to move forward and make progress happen.

13

Finding the Fulcrum

JESSICA CARILLI

My path through and then out of academia was not planned. During graduate school, my fellow students and I actively avoided discussing options for careers outside academia. Many of us felt, naïvely, that obtaining a job outside academia was a sign of failure and only a fallback option for those who could not obtain a position as a professor. Professorial life also seemed ideal, from my hazy vantage point as a student at Scripps Institution of Oceanography. I glimpsed my professors wandering campus lost in thought, stopping to scribble notes on a scree of papers pressed against the back of a van, surfing at lunchtime, walking dogs, or settling babies playing in cribs in the corners of their offices. This all seemed wonderful from the outside: academia appeared to encapsulate the freedom to enjoy life while being intellectually challenged.

Thus, I focused all my energy on becoming a professor. I taught wherever I could, I wrote proposals for funding, I mentored students and conducted service for the University of California at San Diego, and I attended workshops designed to guide students and postdocs into professorships. Then, I continued to chase the professorship dream around the world—first teaching as an adjunct in San Diego, where my husband had a career soft-money research position (100 percent externally supported); then as a postdoc in Australia; then back to San Diego to teach as an adjunct and try unsuccessfully to obtain a full-time position; and finally to Boston, where I landed on the tenure track at the University of Massachusetts in the fall of 2014, five years after graduating with my PhD.

Eventually I realized that my vision of a life in academia was not aligned with my reality, and my career goal of being a successful professor was ultimately incompatible with my personal life. My husband loves his research academic position. He is well-supported by his supervisors and university, has good connections to obtain grant funding, and isn't required to teach. I naïvely assumed he was transportable, but we found that this position was difficult if not impossible to replicate elsewhere.

Both in Australia and Boston, we were unable to finagle a way for him to transition to those places, so we primarily lived apart, visiting one another when we could while trying to minimize disruption to our jobs and disappointment from our colleagues and supervisors. We each felt this disappointment in a variety of ways. We were told outright that our situation was a problem ("You need to physically be here during x, y, and z because of a, b, and c"). We also simply felt that this was why we were ignored (no responses to emails for weeks, for example) or passed up for opportunities ("Well, so-and-so was here, so I asked her to collaborate on the project").

During this time, we also had two children, which brought along its own challenges to our careers, including a reduced ability to travel, restricted working hours associated with child care availability, and, of course, a desire to be present for our kids as parents.

When I got to Boston, I had to restart my academic research career after my adjuncting and parenting hiatus, establish a lab, build new classes, and conduct service—all of which I had some experience doing, but not at this scale. In the meantime, I was extremely time-limited because of my primarily solo parenting responsibilities. I could only devote a little over forty hours to work each week; for me, that turned out not to be enough time to excel on the tenure track. I felt like I was constantly drowning in work, falling behind, forgetting things, and apologizing to everyone. It was also painfully expensive to maintain two houses in different cities, pay for child care for two children, and fly back and forth for brief periods of family unity.

Many of my friends and family marveled at my apparent ability to make this work. I'm glad that despite my own feelings of teetering on the brink of failure, it seemed from the outside that I was keeping it together. However, I don't want to perpetuate the idea that this way of solving the "two-body problem" was somehow a walk in the park. Here's a snapshot of my daily reality in Boston:

- 5:00 a.m.: Wake up, get dressed and ready for the day, check and write emails.
- 6:00 a.m.: Hear the kids wake. Snuggles, clothes, breakfast, art explosions, trying to find the special blankets and lovies and pacifiers and water bottles and snow clothes for school.

- 7:00 a.m.: Load up the stroller, take elevator into the basement, and get everyone into the car. Creep through traffic to day care.
- 8:00 a.m.: Drop off the little one, hugs and kisses, buckle the older one back into his seat, creep through traffic to the University of Massachusetts at Boston, park, walk the older one to the preschool next to campus, hugs and kisses, walk to my office while reading a paper or answering emails on my phone.
- 9:30 a.m.: Teach while feeling bad that I didn't take more time to improve the material, attend meetings where I attempt to contribute but mostly feel like I am crashing a party, chip away at proposals, attempt to keep track of funding without knowing what I'm doing, scroll down to the bottom of my unread emails and send off apologies and promises, feel guilty about not working on research projects.
- 4:00 p.m.: Walk to pick up the older one while working through a stack of grading, bundle into the car and creep through traffic to get the younger one, set them both up with snacks and books in their seats while we drive at near-walking pace through the car-clogged tunnel under the city.
- 5:30 p.m.: Spill into the apartment, reheat something fast for dinner, playing, books, maybe a bath, dishes, cuddles, Skype with dad or the grandparents, bed.
- 8:30 p.m.: Clean up the most egregious messes around the house, tackle bills and laundry and attempt to do grocery shopping online and get overwhelmed and then finish preparing for the next day's class, or more emails, or more writing.
- 10:00 p.m.: Collapse with exhaustion but have trouble sleeping because of the to-do list buzzing in my head.

I didn't mean to leave academia.

I had obtained my goal of reaching the tenure track, and while I was stressed and unsure if I would succeed, I wanted to. This schedule represents doing the best I could at work, while doing the best I could at home. But it was lacking some critical elements: time for exercise, time to read the literature and think of new ideas, time to participate in collegial activities like attending evening lectures, time with my spouse. When he visited, I would swap evening work time to spend with him, thus falling farther behind.

My colleagues were, for the most part, lovely and supportive. They would intermittently come to me offering advice, and help shape my understanding of what I would need to achieve to obtain tenure. Much of the advice was totally in conflict with that from others, or with the way my life worked. I read Hope Jahren's *Lab Girl* and cried because I don't have the physical ability to work without sleep or the drive to live science without infusions of vacation and exercise and friends. Day by day, I felt like the tenure track I was on, which originally had seemed reasonable and fun—like a jog up a little hill—became longer and steeper, more like summiting a mountain.

In light of all this, we had decided that the following academic year, instead of my continuing to struggle to do my job while so much time went to child care, my husband and children would live in California, and I would commute to Boston during the week. This would be hard on me mentally and physically, but would give me more time to devote to my job during the week and would give my husband more time to spend with our children.

Then, we came to an unexpected fork in the road.

My husband was collaborating with scientists at the Space and Naval Warfare Systems Center Pacific (SPAWAR) on a remote-sensing project that would be carried out in a coral reef environment. Months before, I had provided some feedback on their project proposal, so they had learned a bit about my coral reef expertise. More recently, they had learned about our challenging family situation during project meetings. When an impending retirement arose (from a marine scientist who did the primary coral reef work in the group), there was an opportunity for me to take over that position. I looked down both roads and decided that it was time to take a chance and leave academia. Thus completely without meaning to, I leaped off the tenure track and landed in the US Navy.

Despite being essentially unaware of the existence of rewarding and important science careers in the government, I managed to land in one. It has been wonderful and very compatible with my family life so far. I couldn't be happier, and I hope that, by sharing my story, and some I-wish-I-had-known advice, I can help others find their way into jobs like this. My route was serendipitous, but it didn't need to be.

Here is the advice I would have given younger me, had I known that I should be looking into government positions:

Research

There is an incredible array of different government (federal, state, and local) agencies that need scientists, policy folks, and other highly educated personnel. A good place to start would be to go to their websites, research the range of work that they do, and find out whether they employ people with your background. For example, had I thought to look up environmental and natural resources work by the military, I would have found that there are heaps of people doing work that could use people with training like the kind I got at Scripps. I would never have guessed this.

Were I to do this research properly, I would make a spreadsheet of all the agencies I could find that exist in places I might want to live. During my research, I would fill in the sheet with information on what they do that might fit with my background (with links so I could get back to that information at another time). Then I would hunt further for contacts in those particular departments to cold-call, or ideally, I would reach out to my network of colleagues and find out whether anyone I know and trust had contacts and might introduce me.

Networking during a search for nonacademic careers can be intimidating. For one thing, it's a different environment and culture, and it may feel foreign; some suggestions follow in the next section to tackle this fear. Another issue is that it can be nerve-wracking to share the news that you are looking into alternative careers with your academic network; you may be worried you will be shunned or judged. (Sadly, it happens.) Ideally, you would start by discussing your plans with friends and colleagues who have been part of the world outside academia already—perhaps professors who worked for an agency during their postdoc, or grad students who held jobs before returning to school. Those contacts could connect you to their nonacademic network and could help you learn about other agencies or job prospects you hadn't yet considered. You should also come back to them during your reflection phase, described below.

Connect

Reach out to the contacts in your list; I prefer initial contact by email, followed by a phone call if the receiver is amenable, or if you don't hear back from them. The email should be succinct and should let them know you are interested in learning more about the work they do and how their agency is structured and functions. Briefly explain your background and what you think you might bring to their organization. Include a CV or résumé and request a phone call (or meeting if you are local) with them, or someone else in the organization who might be more appropriate, to discuss the job they do and whether you might fit in with their group.

This is not a plea for work; it's an informational interview showing that you are genuinely interested, that you have already done some background research, and that your background is close enough to what they may be after that taking time to talk with you isn't going to be wasted. (In contrast, I've received a vast number of cold-call emails from students looking for academic positions with backgrounds completely irrelevant to my research. They clearly just blasted an email out to a long list of professors in every department without doing any research into what those people do. Don't do that.)

Here's an example of an email that I might send during this phase:

Dear Dr. So-and-so,

I'm currently a postdoc / PhD candidate / etc. at Special University, and am exploring career options outside academia. My background is in Underwater Basket Weaving, and I am intrigued by the work your group is doing integrating specific materials into creating new basket structures. Do you have time for a phone call in the next few weeks to discuss what it is like to work at your agency, and what kinds of opportunities might exist for folks like me in an agency like yours?

Thanks so much for your time,

Jessica Carilli, PhD

It's important here to include more information in this email for the reader to look into—this could be a link to your professional website, or an attached CV or résumé. In the sciences, we use a CV to list our schooling; relevant positions we have held; publications and conference presentations; and other information such as grants received, classes taught, fieldwork carried out, and specific laboratory skills. I would err on the side of including as much information as possible but keep it concise: include many relevant headings that would be left off one-page CVs you might submit for a National Science Foundation grant (mentoring, service, presentations, invited talks, etc.), and populate these headings with information like titles of classes taught, but don't bog down this document with details ("As the leader of this team, I was responsible for blah, blah, blah . . ."). The purpose of including this extra information is to inform the recipients of your email that you have the technical expertise and background skills to be a successful colleague. If they can see this, theoretically they will be more willing to invest time in connecting with you and helping you on your career path.

If you don't hear back after a few days, you can try another follow-up email (so many times things get buried by accident) or a phone call. I might stir up my courage and call, starting out this way: "Hi, Dr. So-and-so, this is Jessica Carilli; I emailed you last week and am just calling to follow up. Is now a good time to chat for a few minutes?" If they say no, you might be able to schedule another time to talk; if you've caught them at a good time, be prepared with a list of questions that you would like to ask (see the next section for some ideas).

My impression so far is that there is far more work to do than there are people to do the work. This challenges much of the chatter around academia, where people have realized that the academy is producing far too many PhDs for the number of open, full-time academic positions. In that case, the supply far outstrips the demand. I believe that in government and probably also the private sector, the opposite is the case. Perhaps this is where the rumor comes from that we "don't have enough scientists," which is used to promulgate the need to inspire more kids to go down STEM training paths but will lead to a rude awakening if they end up seeking ever-more-scarce academic positions.

However great the demand, hiring can be challenging in government. Identifying people who would be a good fit for the work that needs to be done can help agencies navigate their own structures to bring those people on board. For example, a friend of mine identified a branch of a particular federal agency at which she wanted to work because her background fit perfectly into ongoing activities. She contacted the people in charge of the work, and with them crafted a position advertisement for a particular short-term internal funding source. Then, her subsequent application perfectly fit the advertisement and she was hired temporarily, which eventually led to a permanent internal-hiring opportunity. Yet again, effective networking led to a job. Even though it can be intimidating, if you let people know what you're doing career-wise, your connections might be able to help you in some way.

I was hired when I applied to work at SPAWAR through the "New Professionals" program, which selects highly qualified and relatively recently graduated scientists and engineers. Check to see what special programs exist at various agencies. New Professionals are initially supported by overhead funds, and thus can rotate through different parts of the organization until they are selected as a good match for a particular group or project. I submitted my CV through their website and followed up with the relevant contacts my husband had clued me into. Because my background in marine resources, contaminants, and data analysis skills fit many needs at SPAWAR, and a space had been made available by the retirement I mentioned, they were able to bring me in for an interview and then move to bring me aboard. However, because my background is different enough from the bulk of expertise at SPAWAR, I can almost guarantee that had I applied to work there as a shot in the dark, by simply submitting my CV without chasing it up with my contacts, my CV might have been accidentally culled and I wouldn't have ended up being hired.

Reflect

In addition to connecting with folks at agencies to ask about how you might fit into their work technically, it is also important to find out how the work is carried out day to day. That is why informational interviews in person or on the phone can be so helpful. The importance of this information was impressed upon me during my discussions with my now-colleagues at SPAWAR, for which I am very grateful. The work varies significantly from academia, because it is driven not so much by what research questions are intellectually interesting, as in academia, but by the needs of the agency.

These needs will vary widely and shape the work.

For example, a significant portion of work in some agencies may consist not of primary research—gathering and analyzing data—but of technical review of other people's work—such as reviewing environmental impact statements. This work can be intellectually challenging, interesting, and rewarding, but if your passion lies in working in the lab at the bench, it might not be for you.

In addition to the type of day-to-day technical work you would be doing, it's also important to think about other aspects of how the work will be laid out and accomplished. Here are some examples of questions (in no particular order) that would be useful to ask during an informational interview or an email exchange:

1. Will someone higher up give you projects to do, or will you need to build your own path to contribute?
2. Do you need to raise your own funds for your salary through grants and/or direct support funding? Or do you only need to raise funds for research expenses like fieldwork or laboratory supplies?
3. Who does the administrative work, such as tackling personnel issues and tracking spending?
4. Who does the actual technical work? Are there any students, interns, or laboratory technicians, or do Principal Investigators do all of the work themselves?
5. What physical resources (space, facilities, supplies, tools) are available to conduct your work?

6. What is the work culture like?
7. Are working hours strict or flexible? Does anyone telework?
8. What are the benefits like, including pay, vacation time, and so on? (These details might be best researched online, if it is a public-sector job, or asked about somewhat obliquely, such as "Does the compensation compare well with other similar jobs in this area?")
9. Do people mostly work in teams or independently? How are teams built, if they are used?
10. What opportunities for growth exist?
11. What is the best part about your job? What is the worst part?
12. Do you have any coworkers you would recommend I speak with as well? (This could be useful for a different perspective, or to connect with someone whose background might be more technically aligned with yours.)

The answers to all those questions, plus others that you come up with, should be weighed to help you determine whether you would be happy if you ended up in a position at that agency. There is no sense going through a long hiring process if you might just end up leaving soon after you arrive because the work culture is too different from academia, or doesn't suit your lifestyle.

For me, the positives at SPAWAR (important, intellectually challenging work with a clear application, defined hours and expectations, and good facilities and colleagues) outweigh the negatives (the need to obtain all funding for salary, supplies, and travel; the many hard deadlines that seem to arrive quickly; and my lack of understanding of military culture and customs that makes me feel out of my depth a lot of the time). The best part is that I can spend enough time with my kids to reduce my guilt about not being a stay-at-home mother, without feeling guilty that I am neglecting work when I am with them. I'm also happy that (so far, at least) I can stay somewhat on top of the job because the expectations are reasonable and the culture embraces families.

Plus, my job title is literally "scientist," which validates my years of toil in school and training to get here. True, my original goal was to be a "professor," which I am no longer. But when I reflect on why I wanted to be a professor, I see the reason was to do good science, to make a difference in the world, and to be able to live a good life in the meantime. For me, it turned out that being a professor didn't make me, or even allow me to achieve these things; instead, I've reached these goals by becoming a navy scientist. I hope that others find their paths to rewarding careers inside or outside academia, and help to change the narrative of nonacademic careers somehow being a step down from remaining in academia. It's true that I could be counted among those female scientists who "leaked" from the academic pipeline, but I prefer to think now of alternative careers to academia as limbs spreading off the academic trunk, creating a stronger and more full, beautiful tree than one with only one branch.

14

Can I Do This? Do I Want To?

Building a Career in Real Estate

ELIZABETH KEENAN

For the first six months in my current job, people in my office kept asking me, "So, how did you get here?"

It was a perfectly natural question. Real estate is a frequent second career. In the three years I've been in my current job, I've encountered former lawyers, psychologists, furniture dealers, interior designers, graphic designers, and even a film director or two. At the same time, I was fielding another question from my academic friends: "So, are you *really* leaving academia for *real estate*? In New York City?"

That, unfortunately, is also a perfectly natural question.

Real estate—especially New York City real estate—does not immediately come to mind as a natural fit for the post-academic career. Where academia brings status but not much money, New York real estate is perceived as a bunch of lowbrow lowlifes focused on making money with ease. The local stereotype—for example, Donald Trump, or even the brokers of *Million Dollar Listing*—trends toward a flashy broker who excels at selling but doesn't have a lot of deep thoughts. (In the suburbs, another stereotype emerges, in which real estate becomes the purview of the bored housewife.)

And so I heard both the questions from my new coworkers and from my academic pals exactly the same way: How would I, someone who spent the past fifteen years steeped in ethnographic and archival research, who focused on writing and publishing even during a teaching-heavy adjuncting schedule, be able to function in such a fast-paced, deal-oriented, and even materialistic environment? And why would I want to?

Getting Over Yourself

I wrestled with these questions for a long time before I seriously considered a career in real estate. Leaving academia means untangling the expectations that color your sense of self, and chief among them is the idea that *only* a tenure-track job provides the right combination of status, stability, and intellectual satisfaction.

I fell prey to this belief for a long time. For years, as I would complain about my low pay and long hours as an adjunct, my mother-in-law would ask me, "Have you thought about real estate? You'd be great at it!"

I'm not the type of person who hears things accurately. Mostly, I heard, "You'll never succeed in academia! Better do something that requires less brains!"

Enmeshed in my uncharitable interpretation of my mother-in-law's suggestion was the idea that a job had to be high-status and degree-heavy for it to require intelligence or offer any kind of satisfaction. This was me being a complete jerk, because my mother-in-law has a successful career in real estate, does not have a college degree, and is one of the smartest people I know. And, although I never lost sight of her intelligence, I attributed her route in real estate to lack of opportunity: she couldn't afford college; she was a single mom raising my amazing husband; and real estate was a career route available for smart women without other opportunities. So, in a way, I applied the metrics of academia to her life. What *other* amazing things could she have done if she'd had a college degree?

Instead, I should have stepped back and examined my prejudices here, particularly about status, success, and education. From my childhood onward, I conflated a high level of educational attainment with success, or at least what was appropriate success for a Smart Person like me. As I got older, the path narrowed inevitably toward graduate school (because a Smart Person like me should have an advanced degree) and was then further whittled down to the goal of a tenure-track job (after all, as they say, there's always room for people who do good work!). Besides, by that point I had already spent so much time getting the PhD, so much time on my research and writing—why wouldn't I go into academia? Think of all the time I wasted!

In short, I had fallen into a trap that combined snobbery and the sunk-costs fallacy, believing that only a career as an academic would offer me the freedom, as a Smart Person, to explore intellectual pursuits, to write and research what I wanted, and to have rich conversations with other Smart People. But what I never considered was that academia in fact made me deeply unhappy. Yes, I loved my research and writing, and teaching held moments of transcendence, but academia's other aspects were brutal: the expectation of a years-long slog in temporary employment, the required willingness to move anywhere for the chance at a permanent job, the dehumanizing treatment of junior scholars by their seniors and by administrators. Most of the time, these negative qualities meant that I had little to no time for the writing or research I loved, anyway: my contingent status left me unable to pursue most funding for research, and my teaching-heavy schedule meant I had almost no headspace for writing.

At the end of the day, was the trade-off worth it? Some time in 2013, I began to realize that my answer to that question was "No!" And if the answer to that question was "no," I had to ask others of myself: If my desire to be seen as and feel like a Smart Person kept me in academia—a place where I was unhappy—what might it have prevented me from seeing as valid career options? Wouldn't this be a good time to explore beyond the traditional, academia-adjacent careers?

The Search Is On

Like many people leaving academia, I first looked toward the careers that drew large numbers of former academics: editing positions at academic presses, grant-writing jobs at nonprofits, administrative positions within universities. None of these, however, felt like the right move for me. I'd been a longtime freelance editor, so I knew that editing didn't pay very well; I hated writing grants, so making a career out of it seemed like a terrible idea; and, after years of adjuncting, I didn't have a wonderful or rosy view of the administrative bloat that has overtaken many universities.

And so I started talking with people around me in a series of informational interviews. Fortunately, I'm married to a nonacademic, and so I could use his network as well as my own to figure out what I wanted to do with the rest of my life. I worked from our inner circle outward, asking if people would be willing to speak with me about the skills required in their job. It was a daunting task, and many people said no. However, the people who did say yes invariably added something new to my knowledge of life outside academia.

Going into these informational interviews, I already knew I had plenty of transferable skills, from the years of freelance editing mentioned above, to the ability to research practically anything. These skills would fit in *somewhere,* maybe even many places, but I also knew that a lot of those places might not see the fit, or could be unwilling to take a chance on someone who had spent over a decade locked in the supposedly rarified air of the ivory tower. In addition to combating lack of direct experience, I would face the perception that academics are inflexible, too smart for their own good, and generally unqualified to do anything other than write impenetrably about their narrow interests.

Oh, and I'm also a woman. As a white woman, I do not face the level of discrimination that women of color do, but neither was it completely absent (as it was not absent from academia, a story for another time). Sexism shaped the kinds of opportunities available to me, as well as the direction of informational interviews. For example, when I spoke with men in my network—even good friends, and even within academia—I often met with significant doubts about my experience, as well as the relevance of my transferable skills. My past work was never enough, particularly to transfer into fields with "researcher" in the title. My research wasn't quantitative, said one man who had less quantitative experience than I did. My research wasn't ethnographic enough, said another (even though I did nearly three years of fieldwork for my dissertation). Among nonacademic male friends, I found another problem: although several of them had themselves changed careers, they were unable to see me in a role other than "teacher," which was never a way I self-identified.

And so I turned back to the women in my life, who acted both as cheerleaders and as realistic checks on career opportunities. One woman was sure I could break into music journalism, a field she'd abandoned, but then asked why I'd want to take that step backward, given the state of journalism today. I spoke with a friend of a friend in marketing, for whom I'd done some freelance writing. She gave me some great advice about the power of a cohesive narrative to help people imagine you as a good fit for any job, but our conversation also left me feeling like a life in marketing was not for me. And yet another brutally assessed my current career from her perspective as a manager of a real estate brokerage: "Yes, you can make money and have a flexible schedule. And you will have to deal with a lot of stupid rich people."

The women I spoke with weren't acting as mere cheerleaders, but as realistic checks on what their fields had to offer. The difference between men and women was striking, though, because, like the men, all the women had gone through a process of changing careers. But unlike the men, not one woman dismissed my background or skills. The common thread in their advice tended to be: yes, you *can* do this, but make sure you *want* to.

I started to narrow my focus around those two questions: Can I do this, and do I want to?

Weighing the Pros and Cons of Real Estate

Once I started asking that pair of questions, a few priorities started to take shape. I wanted some level of flexibility in my job, both in terms of work hours and what I did. I didn't want every day to look the same, with hours in front of a computer looking at a spreadsheet. Instead, I wanted a job in which I could draw on a variety of skills. I wanted to be in a field where women could excel, both personally and financially. I wanted to be able to pay off the significant debt I had accrued in my years as an adjunct, and some types of flexible careers—like freelance writing—are notoriously ill-paying and time-consuming. (More on the pay and life balance in the final section of this chapter.) None of these desires necessarily defined any one particular career, but they further led me outside the alternative-academic (alt-ac) box.

Real estate appealed to me for a few reasons. Most importantly, the same skills that I honed as a researcher and teacher could be put to good use in real estate. Real estate agents don't just show pretty properties, or make hard sells to investors. Instead, the actual job of a real estate agent includes a wide variety of tasks, from market analyses for proper pricing to writing marketing copy for an apartment listing to researching the history of a house built in 1855. Although I could see how my ability to research quickly and synthesize information would benefit me in my real estate career, my teaching skills were more important when I started the job. Both buyers and sellers needed someone with the ability to assess values, to explain things clearly and calmly, and to act as a sympathetic sounding board. Although I didn't see myself as a traditional "salesman," I could picture myself guiding people through the process and helping them feel that they came to a good decision.

Beyond the transferable skills, real estate offered other enticing elements. Since it's a second career for many people, I wouldn't feel strange or out-of-place jumping in with others when I knew that a significant portion of them had done the same. Additionally, the real estate agents I spoke with (whom I met through my mother-in-law) all pointed out that women made up a large portion of the workforce.[1]

It also held drawbacks, which I had to think very deeply about before I committed (and still think about *all the time*). Most prominently, New York

1. A January 2017 article in the New York real estate trade magazine *The Real Deal* estimated that residential real estate, which I would enter, has a roughly 50-50 ratio of men to women, whereas commercial real estate skews heavily toward men.

City real estate lays bare the inequality in wealth in this country. This inequality plays out across all sectors of the market, whether it's a notice about a new condo going up in Midtown with $25 million penthouses or an all-cash investor parking money in a $750,000 apartment that would otherwise be someone's first home. Gentrification and displacement of communities of color are real concerns throughout the city, and real estate as an industry largely stands in denial of that.

It's easy to lose perspective, too, when working with clients whose income comes from trust funds and inheritances. Early on, I overheard someone in my office say, "It's a real problem when nice, middle-class people making $300,000 per year can't buy a house." There's a lot to unpack there, both in terms of the warped view of $300,000 as a "middle-class" income, and in the very real sense that, yes, many people making $300,000 a year cannot afford to buy a house in New York City. And, while I wanted to make a middle-class income (which I viewed as somewhere above my adjuncting income of $30,000 per year, but far below $300,000), I didn't want to sell my soul in the process.

And about that income: my income in real estate, like my pay from teaching as an adjunct, would most likely not come from a steady source. Real estate is a commission-based industry, which, quite frankly, terrified me. One of the agents I spoke with before entering real estate suggested that I should have at least six months of income saved as a buffer; instead, I had significant debt. Another told me that real estate would be easy, because if your friends and family know, trust, and love you, who else would they use? This statement overlooked that most of my friends had no money, and my family didn't live anywhere near New York City. If I entered real estate, I would be without a safety net, without a network of rich friends, and without truly relevant experience (not the same as transferable skills!).

I almost wrote it off entirely, but then. . . .

Getting the Job

When I took my New York State licensing course in June 2014, I hadn't yet settled on real estate as my next move because of all the cons mentioned above. But I had a month off between the end of the spring semester and the summer session course I planned to teach, and conveniently, Baruch College was offering a compressed, two-week session of New York State's seventy-five-hour real estate salesperson licensing course. If nothing else, I thought, I could get licensed and work part-time for extra income (as though I did not have enough side gigs already during my time as an adjunct).

The course amplified my doubts. It featured two instructors, one of whom was an ancient lawyer in a too-big suit and the other a too-smiling broker who claimed to make $800,000 a year, who traded off depending on the day's subject matter. The lawyer read the textbook, line by line, for 7.5 hours per day, on the days when he taught. The real estate agent barely focused on the coursework, instead regaling us with tales of Decembers spent in Hawaii and the need for suits at all times. And, while I'd love to spend December in Hawaii, I wondered why anyone who made that much money would bother teaching real estate courses as an adjunct, particularly as he didn't seem to love teaching. Within that classroom space, I found it hard to see what the actual job of a real estate agent would look like. There was such a disconnect between the idea of "agency" in real estate (where it means working on someone's behalf) and the self-interest of making a ton of money that I was almost turned off from the whole thing.

And so when my mother-in-law, who works for a developer, offered to help get my résumé in front of the right people at the big firms, I *still* wasn't sure that I wanted to make the plunge into real estate. But I had four weeks of employment left of summer session, and a firm decision not to adjunct anymore. I needed to do *something*. My résumé was out at alt-ac jobs, too, but I kept reaching phone-interview dead-ends with all those applications. To cover all bases (and because I have a hard time saying "no" to my mother-in-law), I gave her my résumé, but kept on pursuing other options.

A few weeks later, I got a call from the corporate HR department of the brokerage where I currently work. Although she had gotten my résumé as a referral from my mother-in-law's company, she had done what she would normally do, which is match my experience to openings. Would I be interested in working in the research department? Or would I prefer to work as an assistant on a team, where I would get a small salary and a percentage on some of the deals? Or did I want to be an independent agent?

For a second, I didn't quite know how to answer her, as these weren't questions that I had anticipated, and the first two options hadn't occurred to me. But, after a decade of fielding questions of all kinds from students, I could think on my feet. *All* of them appealed to me, I said. But because of my transition, a salary would be nice.

Our conversation suddenly made a game plan possible. I had worried the most about how I could possibly survive in real estate before my first closing—and that was after I got someone to buy or rent something, which itself could take months. In either scenario, I would have some income. I wasn't *quite* sure I wanted to be an assistant. One of the women whom I'd spoken to about transitioning had warned me that a general "assistant" title could pigeonhole me. ("Always make sure that there's something before or after 'assistant,' like 'assistant editor' or 'marketing assistant.' Never just general 'assistant.'")

And yet, that's how I started. Within a month of that phone call, after two phone interviews and an in-person interview, I started working on a team in Brooklyn, as an assistant.

A note on personal connections: While my mother-in-law's networking made sure that I got a phone call from HR, it didn't get me the job; my bosses (the two women who led the team) had no idea how HR had gotten my résumé, and we rarely do any business in Williamsburg (where my mother-in-law's developer made his mark). But when someone offers to help, it's best to take them up on the offer.

Surviving the First Year

My brokerage requires its new agents to take a four-week training course before starting in their offices. Assistants aren't required to do this, but my new bosses thought it would be useful for me, since I had no background in real estate.

The training turned out to be the exact opposite of the slick, money-focused licensing course I took. The coursework incorporated a healthy dose of ethics, from understanding the concept of agency to dealing with agents from other brokerages. Experienced agents offered helpful advice on sales techniques in role-playing sessions, and lawyers came in to speak about topics including due diligence and fair housing. I made friends with other students in the class, some of whom already had experience in real estate, and all of whom seemed like decent humans. I finally felt that I was heading toward a "real job," rather than some sketchy industry where people focused on becoming the next Donald Trump (*shivers in disgust*).

Those peer relationships helped me ground myself in my first year, as did the mentorship my bosses provided. Although I felt a little humbled to enter real estate as an assistant, which rendered me invisible to many other agents, I also knew that I had a combined fifty years of experience in my office to draw on. Each of my bosses excelled at different things, which made them a great team, and ideal mentors.

Within a few weeks of starting in my office, I began working with my first buyer—and discovering the transferable skills that would help me find my space in real estate. One of the things that came up constantly in my firm's training was the phrase "educating the buyer," and it's not just elevated wording to make the job seem more legitimate. It's true. Buyers frequently don't understand the process of buying a home. In New York City, for example, I have to explain the difference between a condo and a co-op, and why a buyer might choose one over the other, depending on her circumstances. I guide buyers through a timeline of purchase, from looking for an apartment (the fun part), to getting bank preapproval for a mortgage, to working on a board package for a co-op. Coaching a thirty-year-old through the process of buying her first condo or co-op apartment was no different than working with an undergraduate on her senior thesis.

Once I started working with buyers, I realized something: I *liked* this job. Helping people find a place to live required a set of skills I honed while teaching, but also called on my experience as an ethnographer. I had to listen deeply to what people were saying, what distinctions they made about style and location, and what mattered most to them. It wasn't exactly ethnography, of course, but by figuring out how *they* thought of their ideal apartment, I was better able to help them find it.

About six months in, my bosses assigned me to spearhead a few of their low-level listings. Working with sellers required a whole different set of skills, some of which didn't come naturally to me. Sellers, especially in a "hot" seller's market like the one in early 2015, expected agents to create bidding wars, even on tiny studio apartments. Getting them to face the reality that the apartment they'd bought two years before had not miraculously doubled in value required the kind of patience I once reserved for those students who expected an A, because that's what they always got, but consistently put in C-level work. Only this time the stakes were much higher and involved both real money and not just my reputation, but my whole team's.

And so I worked at keeping calm, patiently explaining the current market, outlining what we could do to try to get the best price. I tried not to feel insulted when sellers wanted to talk with my bosses to confirm pricing, or to make sure that I had done things "the right way." It was like being a graduate student again, only worse, because I was significantly older and wiser, but even more disregarded.

Then I realized something about sellers that made the job easier—and, once again, it had a parallel to those students who demanded higher grades. Most of the sellers I work with are in the process of selling their first homes and buying something else. The transition can be emotionally draining, whether because they're concerned about affording a larger property or because they're leaving a place they love. Like those students freaking out about a bad grade, they were running on anxiety. If I could address the anxiety first, they were less likely to doubt my advice about pricing or to push back against making minor repairs to gain value in the end.

Beyond working with buyers and sellers, I loved the pace of real estate. Yes, I worked six days a week in September, October, April, and May, but I had days when I could leave work early or arrive at 11:00, which left me plenty of time to work on my writing (and even complete a journal article and a handbook essay, finish a young adult novel manuscript, and get a literary agent).

Making a Realistic Assessment, Three Years On

After a year, my bosses came to me with a proposal and, in their eyes, a promotion. I would no longer be an assistant, but I would have more of a back-end role, focused on research, marketing, and project management. I would receive a larger salary, plus a percentage of all deals (not just the ones I spearheaded). The percentage would be smaller, but it would include all deals, so theoretically it would match or exceed my pay at the time. In my eyes, this recast of my job description offered less freedom and less flexibility, and less of an opportunity to focus on the part of my job that I loved—that is, working with buyers.

So I negotiated. First, I successfully argued that we'd had a significant, statistically verifiable increase in sales with buyers since I started working on the team—and that I had been involved in those sales. Second, I agreed to the change in payment but, after doing some back-of-napkin math, at a higher percentage. I wanted to guarantee a pay raise, not sell myself short.

It worked, and the focus of my job moved more toward back-end, administrative tasks and bundles of research. Unfortunately, although I got along well with the women who ran my team, I missed working with buyers and sellers, and I missed the flexibility of making my own schedule. So, after two years of knowing I *could* do a more administrative-oriented job, I decided I did not *want* to.

This decision meant leaving the team and, eventually, moving to another real estate brokerage. This is another step along the journey, and it is somewhat terrifying (though definitely not as terrifying as leaving academia). Being on my own lets me focus on the aspect of the job that keeps me most motivated: helping people navigate a difficult real estate market. But it also means developing other skills that don't come naturally to me, like networking without seeming like Willy Loman.

Not every day in real estate is perfect, and I don't have *tons* of time to write, but I've never regretted leaving academia. It's a lot easier for me to see myself in the fabric of real estate these days, because I know that many of the stereotypes about the field aren't true. I haven't lost my brain or stopped thinking or caring about important things. But I have figured out a sense of balance between financial stability and job satisfaction that academia never gave me.

Epilogue

Unhappy Beginnings

JOSEPH P. FISHER

There is a certain irony that emerges when attempting to write a conclusion for a book that is about new beginnings. My sincere wish, which I suspect is shared by all the collaborators in this collection, is that we have helped you—our audience of budding (or even current!) alternative academics—gain a foothold, to use Lisa Munro's term from earlier, in the disorienting morass that is the career reinvention process. Therefore, I am hoping that most of you have reached this conclusion feeling better about your career paths, wherever they might take you, while also having a clearer sense of how to forge those paths that will either guide you away from academia or will help you find an academic-adjacent position.

In the simplest of terms, I hope that you have reached this conclusion feeling happy.

At the same time, I earnestly want to be sensitive to those of you who do not feel happy about the current—and possibly future—status of your careers. Candidly, on many days, I am unhappy about my professional life. As of the time that I drafted this concluding chapter (summer 2017), I was just over ten years out from receiving my doctorate in American literature. Throughout that decade—and, of course, during my doctoral work as well—I held numerous contingent teaching appointments in various academic departments at several institutions. I also held an administrative position at a four-year institution during that time. However, that administrative position was itself only part-time for roughly seven years of that decade, an arrangement requiring me to piece together an elaborate and ever-shifting mosaic of additional part-time jobs to make a salary that was just under par for a professional in his mid-thirties.

The end result of this strenuous work schedule was that I could never secure significant time to do the kind of research or innovative teaching that would make me competitive on the academic job market. The need to work stopped me from doing the work that I needed to do. Eventually, the field of American literature shifted out from beneath my feet.

More frustratingly, eight years into my administrative position, I was passed over for promotion, because, as I was told, my academic credentials and nearly fifteen years of postsecondary teaching experience did not make me a viable candidate for a career in higher education administration. At no point in the previous eight years, when the institution was benefiting from my work, was I told that I did not have a future in the very office where I had worked for two presidential terms. The university, it seems, exploits students, professors, and administrators alike.[1] Those are the conditions that led me to a multiyear attempt to find employment outside higher education. Those are the conditions that have, at times, made me exceedingly unhappy.

I met the woman who would become my wife in October 1999, two months into my MA degree in literature. We married in July 2005, halfway through my PhD program. We have been married ever since, which makes my relationship, as of this writing, almost eighteen years old. However, I often wryly joke that my romantic relationship with literature is older and longer-lasting than my marriage. That is a fact. I recall quite clearly the spring of my junior year of high school, in 1994, when my American literature teacher made studying American literary culture so compelling, so vital, that I could hardly believe that there was a time in my young life when I did not want to read. From that point, I pursued a series of degrees in literature with a single-minded energetic passion that stood in stark contrast to the dull pickup line that I used to start a relationship with my wife: "Can I buy you a drink?" In 1994, I saw my destiny written clearly on the horizon right beyond the walls of my high school literature classroom: I was going to be a professor of literature when I grew up. I have labored—literally and figuratively—under this delusion for twenty-three years, which is more than 50 percent of the time that I have been alive.

I completed my PhD in spring 2007, which found me making my first

1. Marc Bousquet's *How the University Works: Higher Education and the Low-Wage Nation* (New York: New York University Press, 2008) offers a thorough dissection of the various ways in which universities exploit both professors and students by underpaying them for their labor—their "work"—which, in turn, directly inflates already widespread and severe American economic inequality. The irony, of course, is that a college education has traditionally been viewed as a means to increase personal wealth.

significant entrance into the academic job market just as the number of jobs advertised in the Modern Language Association's *Job Information List* (*JIL*) began a precipitous decline. According to the "Report on the *Job Information List*, 2015–2016," the number of jobs advertised in the English and foreign languages edition of the *JIL* in 2007–2008 was 1,826; in 2015–2016, that number had dropped to 953.[2] It was in the midst of this decline that I was receiving the now-standard advice given to newly minted PhDs: "Take *any* job; move *anywhere*; live apart from your wife of two years because your job is more important than your marriage." At one point, a well-meaning adviser told me that if I was not particularly mobile, I could simply define a commuting radius by car, timing the distances that I was willing to drive, and could then decide to commute by plane to schools that were equal amounts of flying time away. That is, if I was willing to drive two hours to and from work, why not be willing to fly two hours to and from work? To this day, I sincerely believe that there must exist tenured professors of literature who get paid in solid gold bars.

I take nothing away from the decisions that other people have made about their careers. Their business is not my business. Personally, I did not want to live separately from my wife, and I did not want her to sacrifice her career for mine. The two-body problem that Jessica Carilli and Kelly and Chris Baker discuss at length was not a problem I wanted to deal with. (It is worth noting here that I know a minuscule number of people for whom the *move anywhere* advice has actually resulted in tenure-track appointments.) I also think that it is patently ridiculous to suggest that flying to Chicago, and apparently maintaining an apartment there, is the same as driving from Washington, DC, to West Virginia. (Truthfully, driving from Washington, DC, to West Virginia to teach composition and Introduction to American Literature on what would likely be a contingent—or literally a "visiting"—contract might be ridiculous in itself.) None of this advice was particularly helpful—I did not even get offered any of these supposed jobs that were apparently worth *everything* in my life—and none of it made me happy. Eventually, I reached a point where, to paraphrase Elizabeth Keenan, it was clear that I just did not want to do any of this anymore.

So I dissented, and somewhere around 2011, I stopped looking for academic work and committed wholly to my (then still part-time) administrative job that would ultimately not promote me.

2. Modern Language Association, "Report on the *Job Information List*, 2015–2016," MLA Office of Research, January 2017, www.mla.org/resources, accessed online July 15, 2017, 6.

At this point, it might seem that my current unhappiness is directly informed by my past unhappiness and that my unwillingness to follow my advisers' advice is the cause of my continuing disenchantment with academe. I will not entirely discount this perspective. However, as I survey the more than half of my life that has been channeled into an ongoing job search—one that is apparently meant to direct me toward some kind of supposed professional fulfillment—I cannot help but wonder: Why?

Why have I surrendered so much of my present self to an abstract future self that may never exist?

Why have I made my present happiness contingent on future happiness?

Why must I accept, as my previous academic advisers apparently did, academic employment as a totem worthy of self-sacrifice?

Publish, or we must perish, I was so often told. At what point can unhappiness about the terms under which we labor—or the terms under which we labor to find labor—actually stand as an aggressive affront to the expectation that we work at all? Capitalism is an abyss. Why must I gaze into it?

In her antiwork polemic, *The Problem with Work: Feminism, Marxism, Antiwork Politics, and Postwork Imaginaries*, Kathi Weeks traces current understandings of economic productivity in all forms to the asceticism of the Protestant work ethic. Historically, she claims, "Unruly bodies, seductive pleasures, and spontaneous enjoyment [have posed] a constant challenge to the mandate for . . . focused attention to and diligent effort in properly productive pursuits."[3] Her project is to find "subversive potential" in the "insubordination to the work ethic; a skepticism about the virtues of self-discipline for the sake of capital accumulation; an unwillingness to cultivate, simply on principle, a good 'professional' attitude about work; and a refusal to subordinate *all of life to work* [emphasis mine]."[4]

The advice that budding academics often receive, and that I paraphrased above (*move anywhere, do anything; the job—any job—is too good to pass up!*), is ascetic at its core. It demands that nascent scholars become supplicants to the almighty job market, praying that every sacrifice we make—the football games that go unwatched, the families from which we make ourselves distant, the romantic relationships that become strained—will bring us salvation in the tenured afterlife. Any article that goes unwritten, any presentation that goes ungiven, any job position that goes untaken—any of these refusals, the logic would go, could only be made by unfocused,

3. Kathi Weeks, *The Problem with Work: Feminism, Marxism, Antiwork Politics, and Postwork Imaginaries* (Durham, NC: Duke University Press, 2011), 48.

4. Ibid., 77.

undisciplined, and unproductive souls too tethered to the worldly pleasures of the here and now. What is our future worth? *All of us*, we are expected to answer.

For the vast majority of us who never receive a tenure-track position, let alone tenure itself, the natural consequence of this advising logic is a palpable sense of personal failure. The inescapable competition built into a job market that is currently producing fewer full-time jobs annually—not all of them permanent—only inflames this sensation. Surely, in a contest that heated, only the best will succeed. The rest of us are left to feel that our failures are our own—remember the articles we did not write, the presentations we did not give, the jobs we did not take?—because it must have been those moments of unprofessionalism that have devalued us in the eyes of our potential employers. Too consumed by our presence in the present to be bothered with our positions in the future, we have allowed ourselves to be too human—too easily seduced, too spontaneous, too insubordinate—to be disciplined by the discipline of academe. We are, in a manner of speaking, bad students. And, it is implied, we should feel bad about that.

It is no surprise, then, that Ann Cvetkovich has described her life as an academic as one that, at times, has made her feel "dead inside," for it is apparently only when we are our most industrious, our most mechanized—namely, our least human—that we are venerated by academia. Cvetkovich's sentiments about the origins of this dehumanizing deadness are especially relevant for the failed academic job-seeker: "Academia breeds particular forms of panic and anxiety leading to what gets called depression—the fear that you have nothing to say, or that you can't say what you want to say, or that you have something to say but it's not important enough or smart enough."[5] In our imperfect humanness, we—fallen and failed academics—have said too little, and none of it was right, and none of it was, we guess, important or smart. Our words could not conjure the future we desired, and so we are forced to reside in the present at the dead end of an academic job search.

I cannot deny that these are grim words to type and that they are likely grim words to read as well. However, it is vital, I think, to understand that *Succeeding Outside the Academy* embodies two dovetailing narrative perspectives. Yes, heartbreak is a fissure that runs through this volume; at the same time, these essays are ultimately restorative. Each chapter finds the writer moving from a kind of suspended anticipation to grounded action—the

5. Ann Cvetkovich, *Depression: A Public Feeling* (Durham, NC: Duke University Press, 2012), 18.

delayed abstractions of future happiness and fulfillment cast off for immediate professional traction and gratification. Brian Flota, Katie Rose Guest Pryal, L. Maren Wood, and Lee Skallerup Bessette, to cite just a few examples, each describe the demoralizing frustration that academe's employment practices caused them while also emphasizing the sense of empowerment and liberation they felt when they decided, on their own terms, to pursue career paths that offered them a sense of control over their lives and their own *humanity*, to recall Pryal. The writers in this collection, together, have worked to reconceptualize for themselves the disorienting confusion of never knowing their own futures—"you never know," as Abby Bajuniemi pantomimes—into a more concrete consciousness of knowing now what they want and, most crucially, how to get it. These writers have, in Rachel Leventhal-Weiner's terms, reframed success, shaking off the austere vocation-like demands of academe in an attempt to turn—or, maybe even, to run—toward their present professional selves.

Certainly, it is fair to argue that in choosing any kind of consistent economic labor, we are inevitably securing futures for ourselves. That is a fair point. Still, the crucial distinction for us is that the present that we have chosen—or are actively choosing—is one that is not contingent. Our present rejects the contingency of temporary academic labor as a necessary fact of our professional existence. We have denied a career trajectory that demands a progressive series of temporary appointments that can only attempt to build toward a permanent future that every economic fact tells us will never exist.

By choosing the work that we want, we have wrested authority from an employment system that has told us that we must choose the options we are given while never giving us options to choose. This is a small but significant irony—a small but significant subversion. It is the kind of irony that might, say, fashion a conclusion as a kind of beginning—a beginning that could be happening now in a moment that breaks with the past while deconstructing the future. These are the beginnings—exciting, apprehensive, joyful, and sometimes unhappy—that are in this volume. We wish all of you many beginnings like these.

About the Contributors

Rusul Alrubail is the executive director of The Writing Project, where she works on literacy and student voice. She is also a writer, an author of the newly published book *Digital Writing for English Language Learners*, and a social justice activist. Alrubail has taught English composition and literature to high school, college, and undergraduate students for ten years. She has written for *Edutopia, Education Week,* the *Guardian, PBS NewsHour,* the International Literacy Association, *EdWeek Teacher, Teaching Tolerance,* ASCD's *Educational Leadership, Edsurge,* the Annenberg Learner Foundation, Medium, and other prominent education publications. She's a TEDx speaker and a social media influencer on education, race, and equity. Her work focuses on teacher professional development and training, pedagogical practices in and out of the classroom, English-language learners, equity and social justice, and media literacy as a means for professional development. You can find her work on her *Heart of a Teacher* blog: www.rusulalrubail .com.

Abby Bajuniemi earned a PhD in Hispanic Linguistics from the University of Minnesota in 2015. She recently left her post as a visiting assistant professor at Macalester College, where she taught all levels of Spanish language and linguistics. In her new role and career path as a user experience researcher and designer, she hopes to use her background in linguistics to work toward making tech and the content produced for tech kinder, more inclusive, and more diverse.

Chris Baker has been a senior software developer in academia, industry, and government for over fifteen years. Previously a scientist for the US Department of Energy, he developed software for the world's largest supercomputers and published research in leading international journals. At ServiceMesh, and later CSC, Chris worked to streamline development and IT operations for numerous Fortune 1000 companies. He is currently the head of development at Galactic Fog. Chris holds a PhD in computational science from Florida State University.

Kelly J. Baker is editor of *Women in Higher Education* and a freelance writer. She's written for the *New York Times,* the *Atlantic,* the *Rumpus, Religion and Politics, Christian Century,* the *Washington Post, Sacred Matters, Chronicle Vitae,* and *Brain, Child.* She's the author of the award-winning *Gospel According to the Klan: The KKK's Appeal to Protestant America, 1915–1930; The Zombies Are Coming! The Realities of the Zombie Apocalypse in American Culture; Grace Period: A Memoir in Pieces;* and *Sexism Ed: Essays on Gender and Labor in Academia.* She has a PhD in religion from Florida State University.

Lee Skallerup Bessette is currently a learning design specialist at Georgetown University. Before that, she was a contingent faculty member for almost a decade at regional comprehensive public institutions. Her blog, *College Ready Writing,* was housed at *Inside Higher Ed* for a number of years, and she is currently a regular contributor for *ProfHacker.* She has also written for *Women in Higher Education, Hybrid Pedagogy,* the *Atlantic,* and *Academic Coaching and Writing.*

Jessica Carilli holds a PhD in earth sciences from Scripps Institution of Oceanography at the University of California at San Diego (UCSD). She also attended UCSD as an undergraduate, obtaining a BS in environmental systems/earth sciences. Her research focused on coral reefs, climate change, and pollution. She is now a scientist at the Space and Naval Warfare Systems Center Pacific, in the Department of the Navy.

Melissa Dalgleish is a professional and career development specialist who works with graduate students, postdoctoral fellows, faculty, and administrators to develop and deliver individual and group programs aimed at helping graduate-trained researchers find rewarding work inside and outside academia. By day, she supports the 1,200 graduate and postdoctoral researchers who work at her university-affiliated teaching hospital in Toronto, Canada; by night, she works one-on-one with job seekers and writes about PhD issues for *Chronicle Vitae, University Affairs, Inside Higher Ed, MediaCommons,* and *Hook and Eye.* She has a PhD in English from York University and writes and publishes about Canadian poetry after World War II.

Joseph P. Fisher is the assistant director of disability support services at George Washington University, where he is also an adjunct professor of composition and cyber-ethics in the College of Professional Studies. Previously, Joe was an adjunct professor of English in George Washington's English Department and University Writing Program. He was also an adjunct professor of English at the Alexandria campus of Northern Virginia Community College. Joe is the coeditor, with Brian Flota, of *The Politics of Post-9/11 Music: Sound, Trauma, and the Music Industry in the Time of Terror* (Ashgate, 2011). Joe is an RRCA-certified running coach, and he resides in Washington, DC, with his wife, Kelly.

Brian Flota is a humanities librarian at James Madison University in Harrisonburg, Virginia. He received his PhD in English—with a focus on American literature—in 2006 and his MS in library and information science in 2013. He is the author of *A Survey of Multicultural San Francisco Bay Literature, 1955–1979* (Edwin Mellen Press, 2009), the coeditor, with Joseph P. Fisher, of *The Politics of Post-9/11 Music* (Ashgate, 2011), and the current editor of the Association of College and Research Libraries' Literatures in English Section newsletter *Biblio-Notes*.

Joseph Fruscione, PhD, is a freelance editor, stay-at-home dad, and communications director for the nonprofit PrecariCorps. After fifteen years in academia as an adjunct teaching American literature, film, and first-year writing, he left teaching in May 2014 to pursue a freelance career. He's worked as a post-academic consultant for The Professor Is In, and he occasionally does freelance consulting for new alternative academics or post-academics. He's written *Faulkner and Hemingway: Biography of a Literary Rivalry* (Ohio State University Press, 2012) and edited *Teaching Hemingway and Modernism* (Kent State University Press, 2015), among other scholarly writing projects. He's also published pieces about adjunct life and higher ed for *Chronicle Vitae*, *Inside Higher Ed*, *Digital Pedagogy*, *PBS NewsHour*'s Making Sense series, and elsewhere.

Cathy Hannabach is the founder and president of Ideas on Fire, an academic editing and consulting agency helping interdisciplinary, progressive academics write and publish awesome texts, enliven public conversations, and create more just worlds. She hosts the Imagine Otherwise podcast, which highlights the awesome people and projects bridging art, activism, and academia to build better worlds. She is the author of *Blood Cultures: Medicine, Media, and Militarisms* (Palgrave Macmillan, 2015)—which traces the cultural history of blood as it both enabled twentieth-century US imperialism and was creatively transformed by feminist, anticolonial, anticapitalist, and queer artists and activists—and *Book Marketing for Academics* (Ideas on Fire, 2016), which teaches you how to harness your resources, skills, and time to build your author platform and get the word out about your awesome new book. Cathy received her PhD in cultural studies from the University of California at Davis and her BA in gender and women's studies from the University of California at Berkeley, and she went on to teach as a faculty member at the University of Pennsylvania, Temple University, the University of Pittsburgh, and the University of California at Berkeley.

Elizabeth Keenan completed her doctorate in ethnomusicology at Columbia University in 2008. She is currently reworking her academic work on popular music and feminism since 1990 into a book for normal humans. She has published in *Women and Music*, the *Journal of Popular Music Studies*, *Archivaria*, and *Current Musicology*, as well as two chapters in *Women Make Noise: Girl Bands from Motown to the Modern* (Aurora Metro Press, 2012). Her proudest moment is finally getting to interview Carrie Brownstein, for *NYLON*, more than ten years after she tried to interview Brownstein for her dissertation. She sometimes writes for *Chronicle Vitae*, and her occasional blogging can be found at badcoverversion.wordpress.com. Her first young adult novel, *Rebel Girls*, will be published by Harlequin Teen in 2019.

Rachel Leventhal-Weiner, PhD, is the data engagement specialist at the Connecticut Data Collaborative, a public-private partnership advancing the use of open data to drive program and policy decisions. An educator, advocate, and researcher, Rachel runs the CT Data Academy, a public education initiative designed to increase data literacy and expand data capacity in nonprofit organizations, state agencies, and community groups. Before leaving the academy to join a think tank, she worked for nearly a decade in higher education as an administrator, professor, and adviser. Rachel earned her PhD from the Department of Sociology at the University of Connecticut and her master's degree in higher and postsecondary education from Teachers College at Columbia University. She writes about faculty and family life for *Chronicle Vitae*, blogs at www.roguecheerios.com, and cohosts a weekly podcast on gender and gender stereotypes, Boy vs. Girl. Follow her on Twitter @rglweiner.

Lisa Munro graduated with a PhD in Latin American history from the University of Arizona in 2015. She's held a long list of nonacademic jobs, including being a Peace Corps volunteer, a veterinary technician, a medical receptionist in a bilingual hospital office, a teacher, a study abroad assistant, and, most recently, a crime victim advocate. She's also lived in Guatemala and Mexico. She cohosts the biweekly #withaphd chat on Twitter, where academics of all stripes can network and share advice with each other about life outside academia. She's passionate about writing about historical pop culture, archaeology, fake science, critical thinking, the writing process, and the alt-ac life.

Rachel Neff, PhD, has written poetry since elementary school and has notebooks full of half-written novels. She earned her doctorate in Spanish literature in 2013 and completed her creative writing MFA in 2016. Her work has appeared in anthologies and has most recently been published in *JuxtaProse* and *Crab Fat Magazine*. She's a recent Oregon transplant by way of Kansas, Washington, California, Georgia, and Texas. She dreams in two languages and reads in four. You can find her on Twitter @celloandbow. Her business website is www.exceptionaleditorial.com.

Katie Rose Guest Pryal, JD, PhD, is a novelist, freelance journalist, and erstwhile law professor living in Chapel Hill, North Carolina. She is the author of the Hollywood Lights novels, which include *Entanglement, Love and Entropy*, and *Chasing Chaos*, all from Velvet Morning Press. As a journalist, Katie contributes to *Quartz,* the *Chronicle of Higher Education, Paste* magazine, *Dame Magazine,* and more. When not writing, she teaches creative writing and works as a freelance editor.

L. Maren Wood graduated with a PhD in American history, gender, and sexuality studies from the University of North Carolina at Chapel Hill in 2009. Currently, she's the director of research and codirector of educational programs for Beyond the Professoriate, which began in 2014 as a collaboration between Wood and Jennifer Polk. Initially an annual online conference, Beyond Prof is now an online community providing professional development, mentoring, and coaching to PhDs in career transition.

Index

academic job market, 17, 23, 34–35, 139
    family biases, 67–78, 85
    gender biases, 6, 67–78
    hiring practices, 1
    racial biases, 6–7
    sexism, 6, 67–78, 82
    statistics, 1–2, 6–7, 15, 72–73, 172
    See also moving, in the academic job
        market
adjunct. *See* contingent labor
Allison, Marisa, 3
alternative-academic
    careers, 11, 77, 107, 137, 158, 159, 161,
        163
    careers in STEM, 13, 116, 152–153
    gender disparity, 3, 6
    See also nonacademic jobs
Alrubail, Rusul, 4, 139–148
alumni events, 51
American Association of University
        Professors (AAUP), 1–2
American Survey of Earned
        Doctorates, 15

Bajuniemi, Abby, 4, 115–126, 175
Baker, Chris, 4, 73–78
Baker, Kelly J., 1–7, 67–78
Beatty, Kimberly, 27
Bessette, Lee Skallerup, 4, 105–114, 175
Bicks, Caroline, 69

Bousquet, Marc, 56, 171
Brennen, Gregory, 15

campus resources, 19, 36, 50
career
    development, 11–12, 18
    examples, 5, 12, 13, 160
    fulfillment, 138
    graduate-trained, 13
    guidance, 7, 40
    options, 4, 6
    paths, 5, 37, 114
    post-PhD, 12
Carilli, Jessica, 4, 149–158
Center for Teaching and Learning, 110
Coalition of the Academic Workforce
        (CAW), 1–2
community
    building, 63, 89, 101
    online, 94, 112
    outside academia, 7, 59, 112
    turning to for help, 42, 84, 148
Conference Board of Canada, 15
contingent labor, 3, 72–73, 88, 93,
        139–140, 161
    exit strategy, 100, 127
    freeway flier, 103
    impact on women, 3, 72
    low-security, 16, 23, 57
    new normal, 1, 93

contingent labor, *continued*
    not turning into tenure track, 96, 130
    probability of tenure-track hire from, 3, 96
    result of cost-cutting measures, 94
    salary, 23, 45, 98, 102
    thinking will lead to tenure track, 3, 23, 35, 58, 96
    unpaid labor, 98–99
    visiting assistant professor, 131
Cottom, Tressie McMillan, 3
CV
    activities for lines on, 3–4, 76, 84
    assumptions behind, 72
    for nonacademic work, 19–20, 49, 60–61
    to résumé, 28, 29, 30, 100–101
    as sense of self, 3, 26, 67, 68, 71
Cvetkovich, Ann, 174

Dalgleish, Melissa, 4, 11–22
Desjardins, Louise, 15
digital humanities, 108
Drabinski, Kate, 62
dual career, 6, 58, 67–78, 105–106, 149–152

entrepreneur, 6, 33, 146–148

faculty development, 106–109
    feminization of, 113
Female Science Professor, 70
first-generation students, 127–138
Fisher, Joseph P., 1–7, 170–175
Flota, Brian, 4, 127–138, 175
freelance academic, 93–104
freelancing
    commission, 164
    feast or famine nature of, 39–40
    getting paid for, 64, 95, 97, 104, 144
    going full-time, 59–60, 97
    hustling for clients, 99
    pitching, 143
    transition out of contingent labor force, 93, 115, 141

Gainer, M. G., 7
Great Recession, 23, 35, 80, 131

Half, Robert, 53
Hannabach, Cathy, 4, 55–66
hiring practices, 27, 75, 155, 165

Ibarra, Herminia, 21
Ideas on Fire, 55–66
independent scholar, 101–102
industry jargon, 20, 46, 48, 116, 121
informational interviews, 65, 84, 110, 117, 121, 134, 153–155
    example emails, 122–123, 154
    part of career transition, 32, 58, 61, 161–162
    purpose, 32, 33, 62, 87, 133
    reaching out, 31–33, 61
    sample questions, 156–157
    setting up, 50, 58
interview questions, 45, 53, 68, 82, 135

Keenan, Elizabeth, 4, 96, 159–169
Kendzior, Sarah, 96
Kessler, Robin, 29

leaving academia, 11
    feeling of personal failure, 7, 16, 23, 37, 45, 52, 114, 133, 140
    loss of identity, 11, 21, 24–26, 36–37, 46, 54
Leventhal-Weiner, Rachel, 4, 79–90, 100
life
    family priorities, 74, 81, 83
    goals, 37, 39, 40
    outside of academia, 7, 14, 65–66, 73, 78
    priorities, 16, 37, 72, 81, 90, 144
    work priorities, 90, 144–145, 148, 163

Mason, Mary Ann, 71
moving, in the academic job market
    as implied expectation, 17, 74–76, 96, 161, 172, 173

personal experiences, 57–58, 115, 127, 149

Munro, Lisa, 4, 34–43, 170

Neff, Rachel, 4, 44–54
networking, 46, 51, 52, 84, 86, 134
   academic versus nonacademic, 26–27, 153
   asking for references or referrals, 116, 117, 165
   building relationships, 32–33
   changing jobs, 119
   conferences, 135
   connecting, 153, 161
   following up, 156
   meetups, 117, 120–121
   personal introductions, 120, 153
nonacademic jobs
   cover letter, 48, 117
   explaining your PhD, 20, 46–49, 153, 162
   finding a fit, 12, 20, 26, 30, 88, 119, 157, 167
   interviews, 52–53, 116, 123–124, 135
   overqualification, 20, 47, 48, 116
   postings, 20
   recruiters, 50, 118
   search, 26, 27
   struggles, 5, 12
   time it takes to get hired, 33, 49, 118
   titles, 124
   training, 5, 166
non-tenure-track jobs
   affecting women, 3
   perceived as failure, 7, 149
   salary, 42, 45–46

online profiles, 31–32, 50–51
opportunities, saying "yes" to, 63–64, 86–87

Pannapacker, William, 95
parenthood
   choosing over academic career, 105–106, 150

family life in academia (see dual career)
motherhood, 67–78, 80, 105–106, 140–141
   perceived as an impediment to academic career, 85, 96, 140–142
   See also pregnancy
PhD
   imagined idealized life after graduation, 1, 12, 15, 34, 46, 115, 149
   questions before starting, 14
"planned happenstance," 18, 50, 79, 86
pregnancy
   during graduate school, 82–86
   on the tenure track, 150
Pryal, Katie Rose Guest, 4, 93–104, 175

Reed, Matt, 70–71
resources
   Beyond the Professoriate, 23
   Career Linguist, 116
   Competency-Based Resumes (Kessler), 29
   ImaginePhD, 17
   Jobs on Toast, 116
   Lynda.com, 116
   Mitacs (Canada), 19
   MyGradSkills (Canada), 19
   myIDP, 12, 17
   Professional Organizational Development Network, 109
   "Seven Stories," 28
   So What Are You Going to Do with That? (Basalla and Debelius), 12, 17
   Strengthsfinder 2.0, 12
   Strong Interest Inventory, 28
   "The Freelancer," 101
   The Professor Is In, 116
   The Robert Half Way to Get Hired (Half), 53
   "The Waste Product of Graduate Education," 56
   vision board, 28

resources, *continued*
    Working Identity: Unconventional
        Strategies for Reinventing Your
        Career (Ibarra), 21
résumé
    best practices, 30–31, 49
    putting together quickly, 12
    tailoring, 30, 47, 49, 111, 118
Rogers, Katina, 15

salary negotiation, 54, 62, 118–119, 168
Schuman, Rebecca, 95, 100
shadow CV. *See* side hustle
Shine, Jacqui, 95
side hustle, 20, 22, 39, 57, 58, 84
skills, 27
    based on specific knowledge, 5,
        62–63, 129
    communication, 21, 32
    context, 147
    core competencies, 29–30
    development, 14, 18, 58, 60–61
    explaining to nonacademic
        audience, 20, 29
    knowledge, 147
    taking stock in, 16–17, 26, 28, 38, 46,
        47
    tests, 17, 28, 50
    transferable to nonacademic jobs, 4,
        21, 29, 31, 47, 49, 78, 116, 136, 163
    value of, 45, 121, 123
social networks and forums
    blogs, 20, 87, 106, 108, 141
    Facebook, 12, 120, 144
    LinkedIn, 30, 31–32, 51
    Medium, 142
    podnetwork.org, 109, 112
    Twitter, 112, 114

Versatile PhD, 12, 58
Wordpress, 142
    See also online profiles; Twitter
Space and Naval Warfare Systems
    Center Pacific (SPAWAR), 152,
    155, 156, 157

taxes
    "First-Time Freelancer's Guide to
        Taxes," 104
    tax implications of alternative
        academic work, 103
tenure-track
    hires after graduation, 3
    job search (*see* academic job market)
    leaving, 151–152
    requirements, 17
    sacrifices, 17, 149–152, 161
trailing spouse. *See* dual career
transition, 41–42, 125–126, 140, 167
    as a beginning, 44, 90
    career coach, 26, 28, 97, 101
    to nonacademic career, 33, 46
Twitter
    chats, 108, 111
    for finding community, 20, 59, 94,
        106–107, 145
    for networking, 20, 108, 109, 120, 144
    hashtag, 141
    positioning profile for work, 32
two-body problem. *See* dual career

volunteering, 19, 33, 41, 64, 133, 134

Weeks, Kathi, 173
Wood, L. Maren, 3, 4, 23–33, 175
work-life balance, 71, 85, 89, 90, 96, 163
Writing Project, The, 147